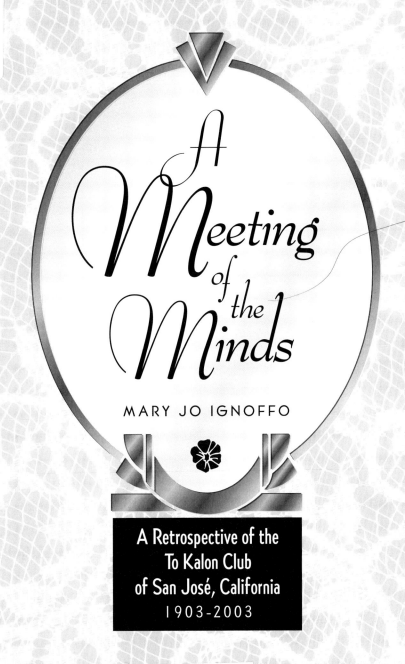

# A Meeting of the Minds

MARY JO IGNOFFO

A Retrospective of the
To Kalon Club
of San José, California
1903-2003

Managing Editor, Tom Izu
Editor, N. Grey Osterud

Published by the California History Center & Foundation, De Anza College, 21250 Stevens Creek Blvd., Cupertino, CA. 95014

Library of Congress Cataloging-in-Publication Data

Ignoffo, Mary Jo
  A meeting of the minds: a retrospective of the To Kalon Club of San José, California 1903-2003/by Mary Jo Ignoffo
     p.cm.
  "September 29, 2003 marks the one hundredth birthday of the To Kalon Club of San José, California" -Pref.
  Includes bibliographical references and index.

ISBN   0-935089-29-2

1. To Kalon Club-History-20th century. 2. Women-Societies and clubs-California-San Jose-History-20th century.
3. Self-culture-California-San Jose—History-20th century.  4. Civic improvement-California-San Jose-History-20th century.  5.  Women—California-San Jose-History-20th century.  6. San Jose (Calif.)-History-20th century.
I. Title: To Kalon Club of San José, California, 1903-2003.  II. De Anza College.  California History Center.  III. Title.

HQ1906.S35 I45 2002
305.4'06'079474-dc21
                                              2002041295

**Funded by the Hugh Stuart Center Charitable Trust**

# Contents

## Dedication

For Elizabeth "Beth" (Crummey) Chinchen 1902–2002 and Helen (Schoenheit) Moore 1902–2002. It was a great honor to meet and hear the reminiscences of two centenarians. And for my friend, wonderful teacher and editor, Grey Osterud

# *Acknowledgements*

TO KALON'S HISTORY HAS BEEN COMPILED to celebrate one hundred years of San José women gathering to explore ideas and culture. I appreciate being asked to document this intriguing slice of history.

Kathi Peregrin, former Executive Director of the California History Center, encouraged club members to pursue their desire to sponsor a publication about To Kalon. She arranged for me to meet Carol Boyce, Huette James, and Shirley Oneal to launch the project.

I was able to interview several club members and hear reminiscences of the club as well as the Santa Clara Valley. I appreciate the time and perspective of each of those interviewed, including Nancy Drew, Huette James, Marion Langley, Shirley Oneal, Masel Sheehan, Betty Wells, and the late Elizabeth "Beth" Chinchen and Helen Moore.

A special thank you goes to those who previewed the manuscript, including Kathi Peregrin, Jack Douglas, and To Kalon's book committee. The manuscript was formally edited by N. Grey Osterud, despite her serious illness.

The San José Woman's Club sponsored the Young Woman's Club in 1903. Diana Wirt, current president of the San José Woman's Club, gave me access to the clubhouse and the early records of that club. The data collected helped to give a context to this history.

Photographs were borrowed from club scrapbooks and a variety of other sources. Paula Jabloner of History San José facilitated my search through original minutes and ledgers. She also arranged for the reproduction of many photographs. In addition, Nancy and John Drew loaned historic postcards. Gretchen Dempewolf of the Sourisseau Academy, and Lisa Christiansen of the Stocklmeir Library and Archive at the California History Center, also loaned images for use here.

California History Center staff members, Tom Izu and Joni Motoshige, have managed the many details of publication with grace and humor. This book has been generously funded by the Hugh Stuart Center Charitable Trust.

In a history like this, it is impossible to mention every club member or every person who has played an important role in the history of the organization. I hope that even those who do not find their names here, can enjoy the story of a vibrant club, and take pride in making it what it is today.

I deeply appreciate the support of my husband, Pat Ignoffo, and my children, Joey and Lisa. They are my treasures.

Finally, I would like to express my heartfelt gratitude to the To Kalon Club's Book Committee. Each member gave time, insight, and support to the efforts here. They are Ginny Brownton, Nancy Drew, Huette James, Betty Kirtland, Marion Langley and Shirley Oneal.

—M.J.I.

# *Foreword*

IN ANTICIPATION OF THE TO KALON CLUB'S ONE HUNDREDTH YEAR in 2003, the membership expressed a desire to hold a centennial celebration and to create some tangible record of its 100-year history. In 2000, the board of directors and the president appointed a committee to work with the club's historian to facilitate a commemorative book to include the history, pictures, and stories of To Kalon.

The California History Center was consulted about the merits and process of publishing a book, and author Mary Jo Ignoffo agreed to write it. She has used minutes, scrapbooks, ledgers, programs, surveys, and interviews to make 100 years of To Kalon come to life.

We are grateful to be associated with this truly exceptional club. We are pleased to present each member with a special commemorative copy of *A Meeting of the Minds*.

*Shirley Oneal (left) and Mary Jo Ignoffo,*
*San José Country Club, 2002*

## Committee Members:

Ginny Brownton

Nancy Drew (Historian)

Huette James

Betty Kirtland (Historian)

Marion Langley

Shirley Oneal

# A Meeting of the Minds

MARY JO IGNOFFO

A Retrospective of the
To Kalon Club
of San José, California
1903-2003

*Woman poses with her motorized bicycle outside the San José Post Office. When the Post Office was relocated in the 1930s, the building became the Public Library. Today it is San José Museum of Art.*

Courtesy of History San José.

# PREFACE

## Now in Session

SEPTEMBER 29, 2003 marks the one hundredth birthday of the To Kalon Club of San José, California. It was established in 1903 as the Young Woman's Club (YWC), an auxiliary to the nine-year-old San José Woman's Club. In 1918, after breaking ties with the older club, the Young Woman's Club voted to change its name to the To Kalon Club. The dictionary defines "kalon" as a form of the Greek word *kalos*, meaning "good, beautiful—the ideal of physical and moral beauty, especially as conceived by the philosophers of classical Greece."[1] The Greek "to" means toward, and the club envisioned itself as striving toward goodness and beauty through intellectual and cultural exploration, a theme that remains a cornerstone of the club's philosophy.

"...striving toward goodness and beauty through intellectual and cultural exploration."

This retrospective of the To Kalon Club has been written as a centennial book to document how the club has evolved over the course of a century. It tells about a group of women gathering to explore intellectual and cultural trends and ideas, and it places that group firmly in the context of San José history. Here we have a window offering one perspective of woman's life in twentieth century California. This story highlights the members themselves, the programs presented, and the places the club met. Club activities and city history are braided together, each giving texture and style to the other.

The history of this club has not been written before, except in very short summaries by those serving as historian. The first official historian, Amy (Mrs. Oliver) Blanchard, was appointed in 1951. However, in 1915, charter member Nellie (Miss) Evans wrote an informal description of the earliest years. Sources for *A Meeting of the Minds* include those summaries, thirteen handwritten books of minutes and three treasurers' ledgers, a collection of printed programs from almost every year since 1903, three club scrapbooks, personal interviews, and a survey of current members (2002).

One frustrating research problem has been determining the given name of many members. Throughout most of the twentieth century, married members were identified by their husband's name, making it difficult to ferret out details about the individual woman. Wherever possible I have used full names and titles. In some cases, the woman's given name was never determined.

Another difficulty is that the club (along with many other organizations, municipalities, and businesses) relied upon the San José *Mercury News* Archives for historical data and photographs. Unfortunately, the newspaper eliminated its entire archive of pre-1985 photographs. The newspaper reported on the To Kalon Club, and before that the Young Woman's Club, almost on a weekly basis. That archive held dozens of To Kalon photographs that no longer exist.

Minutes from 1903 to 1912 are also missing, as are some scrapbooks and clippings from the middle of the twentieth century. Notwithstanding these limitations, a significant cache of records exists to construct a good history. In 1985, club minutes and ledgers were microfilmed and then, along with annual programs, stored for safekeeping at the archives of History San José. Original records and the microfilm copies provided the basis for the research contained here.

From the beginning in 1903, the club adhered to strict parliamentary procedure at its meetings, even seeking advice from the San José Woman's Club parliamentarian. The printed program for the first year delineates the "Order of Exercises." The order included reading the minutes, roll call, unfinished and new business, a paper or presentation, and refreshment. A similar format is followed here to give structure to this story, and each chapter is named for a portion of a meeting. "Call to Order" gives an overview of San José history and the woman's club movement in the United States up to 1903. "Minutes" and "Financial Report" give a history of the Young Woman's Club (and To Kalon), along with its financial standing over the years. The philanthropic contributions of some members are noted in this chapter. In "Roll Call," individual club members and their families are introduced. "Programs" shows the extensive and diverse range of presentations over the years. The YWC and To Kalon has been a club without a clubhouse and has convened at many locations. "Meeting Places" allows a look at some of those venues rich in character and history for the whole Santa Clara Valley.

As this written history faces a figurative "Adjournment," it poses some questions about the future of this and other like-minded organizations. The book is closed in honor of all those who have been members of the YWC and To Kalon. Born of the San José Woman's Club, nurtured by a desire for intellectual stimulation, and carried to maturity by dedicated members, the To Kalon Club approaches its centennial with pride in its interesting past and with hope for a compelling future.

Constitution and By Laws of the Young Woman's Club.

## Article I    Name

This Association shall be known as the Young Woman's Club

## Article II    Objects

To promote acquaintance, good fellowship, and co-operation among the young women of the city, and vicinity; to furnish a stimulus to intellectual growth and culture among its members.

## Article III    Eligibility.

Any young woman resident of this city or county who shall receive the endorsement of the Board of Directors shall be eligible to membership.

## Article IV    Management

The management of the Club shall be vested in a Board of Directors consisting of nine members elected in the following manner; the first year three directors shall be elected for three years, three

*Young Woman's Club constitution, from the first book of Minutes, 1903.*
Reproduced courtesy of History San José.

6

# CHAPTER ONE

## *Call to Order*

WHEN SAN JOSÉ LADIES GATHERED in one or more of the dozen clubs available to them in the first decade of the twentieth century, they carried with them a body of knowledge that is not necessarily familiar to us in the twenty-first century. They were well acquainted with San José and its history. They were very much aware that a strong movement was afoot to secure the vote for women, and many of these ladies had heard public lectures by famous suffragists such as Susan B. Anthony and Elizabeth Cady Stanton. Woman's clubs were so popular that potential members would have understood the workings and purposes of club life.

As the twenty-first century begins, we are not so clear on the popular and social culture of one hundred years ago. This chapter gives an historical overview of San José, summarizes the woman's club movement in the U.S. up to that time, and describes the San José Woman's Club that gave birth to the Young Woman's Club.

> "One way to begin to bring order to a community was through the activities of a woman's club."

### San José

San José is the oldest city in California, founded in 1777 on the banks of the Guadalupe River as a Spanish experiment to colonize Alta California. Fourteen families with about sixty-eight people in all, arrived, built modest adobe homes, planted basic crops and raised livestock. The pueblo was moved slightly to the south shortly after it was established to protect itself from a flooding Guadalupe River. Over the next two hundred years, right up to the present day, the river has repeatedly caused the city to reconsider its relationship to it.

San José remained a tiny backwater pueblo through the Spanish and Mexican eras. With the Mexican War of 1846 and the Gold Rush in 1849, San José suddenly became an important crossroads in California. Gold seekers passing through on the way to the mining territories swelled its population from about 850 in 1848 to almost 4,000 at the end of 1849. San José's location was so important that at California's Constitutional Convention held in Monterey in October 1849, it was chosen California's first state capital. The First Legislature convened in San José in December of that year at a hotel converted into a statehouse, on the site of today's Fairmont Hotel.

San José's tenure as state capital was short-lived, and after four years of indecisive debate in the Legislature, the permanent capital was located in Sacramento. San José's population dipped over the next few years, but increased moderately each decade through the last half of the nineteenth century. The town continued to develop around its old Spanish core—today's Plaza de César Chavez—near the *juzgado* (jail), *la plaza* (the square), and Saint Joseph's Church.

A City Hall completed in 1889 in the plaza remained in use for almost seventy years, although it suffered serious damage in the 1906 earthquake. Facing the plaza across Market Street stood the Post Office, completed in 1892. Thirty-five years later, it became the city library. Today it houses the San José Museum of Art.

There were more than a dozen commercial and office buildings in San José, including the Knox-Goodrich building on South

*Courthouse in San José, built in 1868 across from Saint James Park on North First Street.*
Courtesy of the Sourisseau Academy, San Jose State University.

First Street, the "New Century" building at Second and Santa Clara streets, and the Porter Building on the opposite corner. A number of churches ornamented the town, from the venerable Saint Joseph's Catholic Church to the new First Unitarian Church on North Third Street facing Saint James Park. Nearby was the sprawling Vendome Hotel, occupying twelve carefully gardened acres on North First Street. The Court House (1868) and Hall of Records (1892) stood side by side on North First Street, across from Saint James Park. The Hall of Justice was completed at North Market and St. James streets in 1903 (in the early 1960s, it was deemed unsafe and was razed).

At the turn of the twentieth century, the most conspicuous feature in a panorama of San José was an electric light tower. Located at Santa Clara and Market streets, it shed 24,000 candle-power, stood well over two hundred feet tall, and weighed fifteen tons. It lit up the immediate vicinity, but never illuminated the outlying neighborhood as promised by its promoters. The tower gave San José a distinctive skyline, and town boosters featured it on their promotional literature and picture post cards. San José was the first city west of the Mississippi to be lit by electricity, and was fond of boasting about that fact. Unfortunately, the looming electric tower toppled after a severe wind storm in December 1915. A half-sized replica stands today at History San José in Kelley Park.

San José was home to some important educational institutions. The College of the Pacific (today's University of the Pacific in Stockton, California) was a Methodist-founded

*San José's Electric Light Tower, circa 1890s, which stood at Santa Clara and Market streets for thirty-four years beginning in 1881. San Jose was the first city west of the Mississippi to be lit by electricity.*
Courtesy of the Sourisseau Academy, San Jose State University.

*San José's State Normal School, circa 1870s, facing Fourth Street.*
Courtesy of the Sourisseau Academy, San Jose State University.

*Graduation at San Jose Normal School's inner quadrangle, 1912.*
Post card courtesy of Nancy & John Drew.

academy for both men and women. Its school was in the College Park neighborhood of San José, today's campus of Bellarmine College Preparatory High School. The Methodist college played an important role in Santa Clara County, schooling many civic and social leaders.

California State Normal School at Washington Park, today's San José State University, graduated its first class of teachers in 1872. The San José *Mercury and Herald* often reported on events at the school and nicknamed the students there as the "Normalites." The original structure, which burned in 1880, was replaced by a building designed by San José architect Levi Goodrich. This second building succumbed to the 1906 earthquake, and was replaced by a masonry quadrangle. Tower Hall on today's campus is the only remnant of the early campus. Many YWC and To Kalon members were alumnae of San José State.

On the same property at Seventh and San Fernando streets, and part of Washington Square, stood San José High School. It was also destroyed in the 1906 earthquake. It was rebuilt at the same location and remained there until the university took it over in the early 1950s. It reopened at Julian and Twenty-fourth streets.

Notre Dame Academy was a Catholic girls' school that had been established first in Santa Clara during the 1850s, then in San José. It had a reputation among the wealthier residents of the valley as the best school for daughters on "the brink of womanhood." Catholics and non-Catholics alike, chose Notre Dame to send their daughters for a formal, disciplined, and classical education.

San José boasted a few distinctive attractions for visitors to California. Among them was Lick Observatory, named for James Lick and opened in 1888 atop Mount Hamilton, on the south rim of hills surrounding Santa Clara Valley. The observatory was the first of its kind, and when its giant 36-inch telescope was installed in 1888, it was the largest in the world. The telescope was used for astronomical discoveries and has been a source of pride to the county ever since. Early in the twentieth century Lick Observatory was a very popular destination, and it remains open today, attracting visitors from all over the world.

Over the years, San José welcomed the most powerful political leaders in the land. President William McKinley gave a rousing speech in Saint James Park in 1901, just four

*Lick Observatory and its giant telescope, a popular destination for visitors to San José.*

Photograph from *The Road of A Thousand Wonders*, a 1908 publication of the Southern Pacific Company.

*United States President William McKinley greets Mrs. E. O. Smith, a local leader of woman's groups, at his visit to Saint James Park in San José.*

Courtesy of History San José.

*President Theodore Roosevelt on a visit to Santa Clara County, planting a tree, circa 1903.*

*Annex to the Vendome Hotel after the 1906 earthquake.*
Courtesy of the Stocklmeir Library and Archives, California History Center.

months before he was assassinated in New York. His visit and a monument erected in his memory drew dozens of San José socialites into the public venue to solicit funds and manage social events. President Theodore Roosevelt visited the valley in 1903, staying at the Vendome Hotel, and touring Alum Rock Park, Lick Observatory, Congress Springs, Big Basin, and some private homes. He was photographed planting trees at various locations around the valley.

The 1890s were the heyday of fraternal organizations. Among the groups in San José were the Odd Fellows and its female counterpart, the Rebecca Lodge; the Knights of Pythias; the Native Sons of the Golden West; the Masons and female auxiliary the Eastern Star; the Catholic Knights of Columbus (Italian); and Ancient Order of Hibernians (Irish). An exclusive businessmen's club, the Sainte Claire Club, built a clubhouse across from Saint James Park in 1894. That same year, the San José Woman's Club was founded.

The 1906 earthquake wreaked havoc in San José and put several buildings out of commission. The Porter Building was so damaged that it remained closed for many months after the quake. Many local vendors and retailers lost inventories and shop space in the quake. Artist and photographer Andrew P. Hill, who had a studio in downtown San José, lost practically his entire stock of paintings. The three-year-old annex to the Vendome Hotel crumbled, and a guest was killed. San José High was destroyed along with the main building at the State Normal School. It took a couple of years for the city to recuperate from the trembler.

Across the broad Santa Clara Valley, large Spanish land grants had been sold and subdivided in the 1880s, and ten to forty-acre fruit orchards cropped up in every direction. One of the more prestigious residential areas was along the Alameda, on the way to Mission Santa Clara. Large, expensive homes were built along the willow-shaded street. The economy was firmly entrenched in fruit orcharding, processing, and shipping, and the fruit canning industry was just coming into its own. Within the first two decades of the twentieth century, Santa Clara Valley was dubbed the "Valley of Heart's Delight" because of the produce of its millions of fruit trees. The valley was gaining a world-wide reputation for the tons of dried fruits shipped out of the county.

The city and county took great pride in being known as the Valley of Heart's Delight. Annual blossom parades were held in several locations each year. The *Fiesta de las Rosas*, the largest parade in San José, was held annually in May. Floral-decorated floats carried costumed young ladies depicting mythical nymphs and fairies. In the late 1920s, at the urging of Cora (Mrs. Fremont) Older, the city of San José set aside five-and-a-half acres as a Municipal Rose Garden. Dedicated in 1937, it held four thousand rose shrubs of 189 varieties. At the time, the rose garden appeared to be on the extreme fringe of the city.

*Annual Grecian celebration held in May at San Jose Normal School, circa 1911.*

Post card courtesy of Nancy & John Drew.

*Two women pose at the Municipal Rose Garden in San José, 1947. The Rose Garden neighborhood is visible in the distance.*

Courtesy of History San José.

*A view of Santa Clara Street, San José, circa 1959. Hart's Department Store, a popular store for decades, is center.*
Courtesy of History San José.

*Postcard advocating woman's suffrage in California.*
Courtesy of the Stocklmeir Library and Archives, California History Center.

Today, a prominent Rose Garden neighborhood surrounds the city-owned garden.

San José was the site of California's last public lynching in 1933. A popular young heir to the Hart Department Store business had been kidnapped and murdered. A horrified San José reacted with swift vengeance when hundreds of townspeople stormed the jail and dragged the two accused kidnappers to Saint James Park and hanged them. No one was ever brought to trial for the lynching. In fact, for more than fifty years, no witnesses came forward, even though hundreds of people were at the park that night. The incident has remained controversial, and rarely is there a consensus on its ethical dimensions.

After World War II, San José experienced a huge population boom like the rest of California. Inventions and research from the war gave birth to the electronics industry in the Santa Clara Valley. The City of San José hired Anthony P. "Dutch" Hamann as City Manager, and his aggressive policies reshaped San José. Envisioning the valley as "the Los Angeles of the north," he was both lauded and criticized for his unabashedly pro-growth stance. The "Valley of Heart's Delight" became the "Silicon Valley."

## Women's Clubs

By the time the Young Woman's Club was founded in 1903, the women's rights movement in the United States was already over fifty years old, having its genesis at the world's first such convention in Seneca Falls, New York in 1848. But female groups had been gathering in America as early as the establishment of the Massachusetts Bay Colony when they discussed the weekly religious sermons. Later, the groups became stitching circles, and much later, missionary support groups and temperance advocates. From the beginning, women's groups found both critics and supporters among men.

The abolition movement before and after the Civil War inspired passion in many sectors of American society. Some women stepped out of traditional roles to try to make an impact on national abolition policy by public speaking engagements to persuade others to adopt their point of view. Scholars have pointed out that after the Civil War, women took on the task of making social order in the country. Many traditional household tasks such as bread-baking, soap-making, and sewing, were no longer performed in the home, but in factories and department stores. Hot and cold running water became the norm, and it was no longer necessary to haul water from a well. Women had more leisure time than ever before. They had been successful managing their homes, so they brought their skills out into society, to a larger forum. One way to begin to bring order to a community was through the activities of a woman's club.

The National Woman's Suffrage Association, established in 1869, specifically aimed at adding an amendment to the Constitution ensuring a woman's right to vote. The Woman's Christian Temperance Union (WCTU), an anti-alcohol coalition established in 1873, had local chapters in Santa Clara County by the 1880s. Many clubs had roots in the WCTU, and some became study clubs. Often these evolved into civic improvement groups, sponsoring public libraries and community beautification. By the 1930s, many of the clubs focused on literacy campaigns, art projects, or concert sponsorships. Neither the San José Woman's Club nor the To Kalon Club followed these patterns precisely, but both were influenced by the national trend in woman's clubs.

Late in the 1890s, the San José *Mercury and Herald* devoted several pages each week to the woman's club movement in the United States. It gave the latest club news from cities like Boston, New York, and New Orleans. It ran articles headlined "Gossip

*Advertisement for a "Suffrage Doll."*
Courtesy of the Stocklmeir Library and Archives, California History Center.

*Interior of typical turn-of-the-twentieth century home. This was the Bray home in Santa Clara. Current member, Marion Langley, is a descendant of the Brays.*
Courtesy of History San José.

of Women's Clubs," and "Shall Men Choose Women's Clothes?" That article concluded that men should indeed choose women's clothes, but that likewise, women were better at choosing men's clothing.[2] The paper also carried more serious debates on women's clubs. "Do Women's Clubs Injure the Churches?" claimed that clerics were distressed because women were no longer devoting themselves to church work, but diverting their efforts to club activities. One woman protested that "women have advanced sufficiently to demand the rewards of work, a fact which the churches are too slow, for their own good, to recognize."[3] The article made it sound as if the churches missed the women's work, not necessarily the women themselves.

By the turn of the twentieth century, the American woman's club movement was at its zenith. A comprehensive history of the movement authored by Jane Croly, entitled *The History of the Woman's Club Movement in America*, published in 1898 may have served as a resource for the new club in San José. Croly had been the founder of Sorosis, an early New York City woman's club. One historian points out:

> Although estimates vary, it is reasonable to assume that well over two million women participated in the club movement at the turn of the century, and since most of these women interacted, as daughters, mothers, sisters, wives, or friends, with a circle of others, club influence extended to a good portion of the population.[4]

In San José, as in other clubs across the nation, a club member would often invite her friend, sister, daughter, or daughter-in-law to join.

Clubs drafted bylaws and constitutions to set the focus for club activities. In some cases the emphasis was on suffrage and politics, others pursued study or community service. At first the clubs met in private homes; as membership grew, they moved to a public meeting room at a library, city hall, or church. Only well-established clubs successfully collected funds and built their own clubhouses. The YWC rented space in a commercial building.

Both the San José Woman's Club and the YWC were dues-paying members of The General Federation of Woman's Clubs. Each club also joined the state federation. Typical of most of these clubs, and true of the two local ones, was setting "departments," or small focus groups. "By 1906, five thousand local organizations had joined the General Federation of Woman's Clubs," probably only five to ten percent of actual clubs in existence.[5] California extended the right to vote to women in 1911, and in 1920 women got the vote nationwide. After 1920, the National American Woman Suffrage Association recast itself as the League of Women Voters, an organization that carries on today.

*Refreshment booth at a July Fourth celebration at Saint James Park in San José in 1909. The booth was staffed by local women.*

Courtesy of History San José.

## The San José Woman's Club

On a December afternoon in 1894, nine women[6] met in the South Second Street studio of Fannie (Miss) Estabrook, a speech instructor at College of the Pacific and later at San José Normal School, to form the San José Woman's Club. The club's goals were to "promote acquaintance, good fellowship and cooperation among women of this city and vicinity, to furnish a civic center where all questions of importance to the community might be freely discussed and acted upon, to afford an agency through which helpful and

*East Hall of University of the Pacific while it was located in San José. Several Young Women's Club members were students at the Methodist-based school.*
Courtesy of History San José.

uplifting influences may be extended."[7] The group quickly recruited new members and they began meeting in Pythian Hall on Second Street, in the same building as Estabrook's studio. Among the women important in forming the San José Woman's Club was Catherine (Mrs. E. O.) Smith, who presided at most of the meetings until after the third year when an official president was chosen; Louise C. (Mrs. Stephen) Jones, the first official president of the woman's club; Katherine (Mrs. William C.) Kennedy, president in 1903 when the YWC was formed; and two women who had daughters in the YWC, Carrie Stevens (Mrs.) Walter and Helen (Mrs. Dr. Leonard) Stocking.

Mrs. E. O. Smith was "very much in society,"[8] and according to Bertha Rice's 1955 book, *Women of Our Valley*, Smith was "the acknowledged leader of womens' [sic] activities in San José at that time."[9] She was chosen to greet President William McKinley during his visit to San José. She died in 1904. Katherine (Mrs. William C.) Kennedy, whose husband was a prominent attorney, was president of the San José Woman's Club when the YWC formed in 1903.

Louise (Mrs. Stephen) Jones was the first official president of the San José Woman's Club, serving from 1898 through 1900. She had worked as a journalist during the late 1870s when she followed the Rutherford B. Hayes presidential campaign around the country as a reporter. She and her husband had lived in several places, including Germany and the state of Nevada, where he had been the president of Nevada State University.

The Joneses moved to San José in 1894, the same year that the woman's club was established. They lived in the College Park neighborhood of San José, and attended the tiny Quaker meetinghouse on Morse Street, which still stands today. Louise was active in many causes, including temperance, education for blacks and Indians, and the Big Basin save-the-redwoods campaign that started the Sempervirens Club. She wrote many articles about these issues. The Joneses had two sons: the Reverend Augustine Jones and California State Senator Herbert C. Jones,[10] who was often a guest speaker for the To Kalon Club in the 1930s and 1940s.

Carrie Stevens Walter was a poet and journalist and she was married to a newsman too. She was one of seven founders of the Sempervirens Club which saved Big Basin, a grove of old-growth redwoods that became California's first state park. Her daughter, Mary Walter, taught at San José Normal School for a short time, and also became a well-known editor of the children's page of the San Francisco *Bulletin*. Mary joined the Young Woman's Club, but her mother, Carrie, died in 1907 at age 67.

Helen Stocking was the wife of Doctor Leonard Stocking, the superintendent at Agnews State Hospital. She was active in the San José Woman's Club, and served as a liaison for the YWC. Their daughter, Helen Stocking, was a drama student at San José Normal School and became a member of the YWC.

The woman's club adopted the motto "one for all, and all for one," chose the California poppy as it official flower and designated yellow as its symbolic color. In 1902, each of the nine club founders became a director, in charge of a particular committee or "department," and membership surged along with support to procure a clubhouse. The following year, the club agreed to launch an auxiliary for their daughters and the young women of San José.

*Carrie Stevens Walter, journalist, environmentalist, and member of the San José Woman's Club. Her daughter, Mary Walter, was a member of the Young Woman's Club.*
Courtesy of History San José.

Oct 17, The regular weekly meeting of the Young Woman's Club was held on the above date at the home of Mrs. Maud Miller Graves, the President, Miss Dorothy Donovan, presiding. At the business session, the resignation of Mrs. Lownsberry was read and accepted.

Mrs. Graves favored the club with an instructive paper on "Women of the Ancient World," describing the status of the Hebrew, Persian, Egyptian, Greek and Roman women and entertainingly reading excerpts from Eber's "Egyptian Princess" and Ferrero's "Women of the Caesars."

Tea and cake were served on the veranda.

Ada Jane Kimball,
Sec,

# CHAPTER TWO

## Minutes

IN THE FALL OF 1903, an auxiliary of the San José Woman's Club was formed made up of the daughters of members of the woman's club. The daughters were allowed to ask one friend to join. The Young Woman's Club (YWC) had forty-eight charter members. The newspaper reported that:

*"As we think, so we become."*

> A young woman's auxiliary to the Woman's Club is now being organized and fifty names have been signed on the charter roll. The auxiliary will give a university extension course and take up practical work. The auxiliary will bring the younger members of society in contact with the matrons and be the means of materially strengthening the club.[11]

The young women chose the color gold, mirroring the senior woman's club yellow. They settled on violets as their official flower. The club was formally formed on September 29, 1903, when a constitution and bylaws were agreed upon. The club decided to meet Thursdays at 2:30 in Room 61 of the Porter Building.

The purpose of the club was slightly different from that of their mothers'. It was "to promote acquaintance, good fellowship and cooperation among the young women of the city and vicinity, and to furnish a stimulus to intellectual growth and culture among its members."[12] It emphasized intellectual growth and culture over civic improvement, which could reflect a desire on the part of the mothers to expand the horizons of their daughters with knowledge and culture. A second, although unofficial purpose was articulated by one member: "the members hoped to bring out latent talent, encourage extemporaneous remarks, and cultivate expression."[13]

The YWC did not purport to be a civic group, nor did it advocate suffrage or women's rights. Rather it was established as an educational group, or study club. The club year was based on an academic year, in imitation of college life. Nevertheless, the club still demanded a lighter load than a college course of study which, at that time, often required a classical language like Latin or Greek, as well as science, literature, and mathematics. Club activities were curtailed in summer, to allow young mothers time with children on vacation from school.

A theme was established for the year, and the meetings and programs were designed around that theme. Serious planning and significant effort went into program planning. For the first decade, the members themselves or directors from the woman's club presented carefully prepared papers. Guest speakers also made occasional appearances. The programs for the first year focused on European language, art, literature, and music. Louise (Mrs. Stephen) Jones presented one program on German literature, drawing on her time spent living in Germany. But most of the programs were papers presented by the young women themselves.

Of the forty-eight charter members, 42 were unmarried. Most members lived in central San José, with a few in the outlying areas of Santa Clara, Los Gatos, or Milpitas. About half had mothers in the San José Woman's Club, all were Caucasian and had high educational expectations. Among their fathers were two physicians, a railroad manager, a department store owner, an orchardist, the president of College of the Pacific, a jeweler, two attorneys, a journalist, and an undertaker.

The first president of the YWC was Genevieve (Miss) Chambers, whose mother was a woman's club member. Her family moved out of the area within a short period by 1904. The first corresponding secretary, Celia (Mrs. Everett) Bailey, left handwritten notes stating that between ten and fifteen young women regularly attended meetings and events the first year. The number of charter members far exceeded the weekly attendance.

The original charter members were:

| | | | |
|---|---|---|---|
| Mrs. Maud Archer | Miss Mabel L. Dorsey | Miss Ethel Kirk | Miss Edna Rinn |
| Mrs. Amy Gregory Blanchard | Miss Harriet Tigue Easton | Miss Edith Kirk | Miss Helen Stocking |
| Mrs. Maud Gilchrist | Miss Nellie Evans | Miss Florence Latta | Miss Ella Saunders |
| Mrs. Georgine F. Bean | Miss May Evans | Miss Edna Latta | Miss Edith Stahl |
| Mrs. Celia Wilbur Bailey | Miss Margarite Dinsmore | Miss Edith MacChesney | Miss Katherine Stahl |
| Mrs. Eve Chamberlain Biddle | Miss Genevieve Goodacre | Miss Maude McClish | Miss Ethel White |
| Miss Ruby Brooks | Miss Edith Granger | Miss Ione MacLouth | Miss Georgie Willey |
| Miss Ella Brady | Miss Florence Granger | Miss May Morton | Miss Jane R. Williams |
| Miss Bessie Conkey | Miss Florence Haas | Miss Jeanette Noble | Miss Mary Walter |
| Miss Genevieve Chambers | Miss Edith Hoch | Miss Hope Pyburn | Miss Grace Woodrow |
| Miss Dorothy Cain | Miss Stella Kuhn | Miss Maude A. Rogers | |
| Miss Louise Caldwell | Miss Mignionette Kuhn | Miss Augusta Rinn | |

The format was somewhat more formal at the beginning. It entailed reading the minutes, roll call, business both new and unfinished, a recess, presentation of paper, and a round table discussion, finishing off with current events.[14] The young women were divided into "departments," including art, literature, music, history, languages (German and French), and household economics. There is no doubt that the club emphasized education. In reviewing the history of the club in 1916, member Nellie (Miss) Evans reported that "in the beginning, the program for one year was almost an attempt to cover a college course of study."[15]

The club motto also reflected this attitude: "As we think, so we become." Similar to mottoes of other women's study clubs across the nation, it reflected the notion that self-improvement would lead to progressive social and civic improvements. After all, the enlightenment of women would certainly improve men's world as well.

One of the first public events in which the club participated was "Blossom Day" held on April 7, 1904. The newspaper noted that:

> This procession, a bewildering mass of color, a succession of prancing steeds, towering floats, and vehicles of all kinds and sizes, almost unrecognizable from the masses of drapery, greenery and flowers, moved along East Santa Clara Street...thence to Agricultural Park. All along the route the crowds on the sidewalks and street awaited its passing and manifested their approval of the varied features by applause.[16]

The Young Woman's Club members paraded on floats and cars, and a small group rode in the club-sponsored tallyho, "trimmed with poppies, denoting gold, the color of the club."

The following year, club members were active participants in a June festival at Agricultural Park, the popular name for the seventy-six-acre county fairgrounds on The Alameda near Hester Avenue. Many events were held there, including horse, bicycle, and eventually, auto races, circuses and other big attractions. The park had a large pavilion with a grandstand and a grove of shady trees. Opening day that June brought 2,000 people, with a children's parade with over 100 youngsters. Dozens of booths displayed local goods, and a Hawaiian booth was "womaned," as the newspaper put it, by YWC members Misses Edith MacChesney and Florence Granger. In the afternoon, a baseball game pitted the local members of the bar association against the medical profession. The doctors won. The highlight of the day was the "grand baby show," displaying carefully groomed infants of the ladies of San José. In the evening, music and dancing lasted until midnight.[17]

The addition of an auxiliary of young ladies to the woman's club was not entirely welcome. Evidently Katherine (Mrs. William C.) Kennedy, president of the San José Woman's Club, objected to how the new young women were managed, and her concern was specifically directed at Helen (Mrs. Dr. Leonard) Stocking. Some details of that early conflict are spelled out in notes written by Celia (Mrs. Everett) Bailey. She wrote in February of 1904:

*A horse-drawn wagon of San José ladies in a parade headed south on First Street, July 4, 1914.*

Post card courtesy of Nancy & John Drew.

The Woman's Club has just gotten into a muddle over the Advisory Representative of their club in our auxiliary club. Their president tried to put out Mrs. Stocking, our advisory head, of whom she is jealous. Those women's quarrels are tiresome. But Mrs. Stocking has consented to stay & things are calm again.[18]

The club struggled with how to manage its membership. Some charter members had moved away or resigned from the club. In 1908, there were a surprising fifteen new members. Before a woman was allowed to be a member, her name had to be presented to the directors. If the directors voted to approve, then the name was forwarded to the general membership where it was voted upon. Three nays could keep a person out of the club. "A critic was appointed to report mistakes and irregularities so that the highest standards would be kept."[19]

Rules had to be applied equally to all. In 1913, the club voted that a member's name would "be dropped from the roll upon being absent four consecutive meetings without sending an excuse to a director."[20] In fact, it was not too long before "two names were dropped on account of not complying with rules and regulations of the club."[21] At the same time, a proposal was made to create a category of associate members. Three years of active membership was required before one could qualify.[22] Associate membership, which allows someone to keep contact with the club when they are no longer able to be active, is still implemented today. Honorary membership was also established to accommodate some who had made significant contributions to the club. By 1940, there were twenty honorary

Notations made by Celia (Mrs. Everett) Bailey in 1904.

members but by the early 1970s, the honorary list became so cumbersome that this category was eliminated.

Sometime between 1913 and 1917, the Young Woman's Club gradually became independent of the San José Woman's Club. Although there is no direct mention of an official separation in the minutes, the new group became more autonomous. One clue is that as early as 1913, discussions were held about changing the name of the YWC.[23] A committee of six was formed to consider new names, but no more discussion shows up in the minutes for almost five years.

Another symptom of a change in the relationship is that the YWC ordered its own stationery in 1915. The minutes from a director's meeting noted that "it was thought advisable for the club to have their own stationery"[24] headed "Young Woman's Club San Jose." Evidently, the club had not previously used its own stationery, but had relied on the woman's club for such supplies. The two clubs still cooperated on some projects. Later in 1915, the YWC agreed to "provide a few [musical] numbers for the Woman's Club program."

A newspaper interview over fifty years later in 1971 indicated that while Effie (Mrs. Harold) Hunt, Grace (Mrs. Harvey) Herold and Hazel (Mrs. Mark) Hopkins, three longtime To Kalon members were reminiscing, they indicated that the original group broke off from the woman's club because it wanted to be more independent.[25] Others thought the newer group did not want to fundraise for a clubhouse.[26] In any case, the relationship between the two clubs faded, and eventually members of each club were largely unaware of previous connections.

In 1918, another committee to suggest new names consisted of Laura (Miss)

*Armistice Day parade in San José in 1918. The flag is carried by "Liberty Girls," some belonging to the Young Woman's Club.*

Courtesy of History San José.

Bailey, Cora H. (Mrs.) Johnston, and Clara (Mrs. Warren) Reilly.[27] Among the names suggested were the Coterie, California Club, Addams, Sequoia, Sorosis, Sempervirens, To Kalon, *Las Hermanas* (the sisters), and Thursday Study Club. The decision was made at the spring picnic at Edna (Mrs. Arthur) Curtner's in 1918. It took two ballots.[28] On the first ballot, "To Kalon" received nineteen votes; "Young Woman's Club" and "Las Hermanas," each got eighteen votes. On the second ballot, To Kalon received twenty-seven votes to Young Woman's Club's sixteen. It was decided. From that day forward it was known as the To Kalon Club, the Greek phrase for striving toward goodness and beauty.

To Kalon began to redefine itself during the late 1920s and there was clearly a trend away from the educational emphasis of the early days of the club. Although all evidence confirms that the YWC started out as a study club, an emphatic denial of that is taken from a club report. It claims:

> To Kalon was not organized as a study club. The object of the Club is to promote acquaintance—good fellowship, cooperation among its members, and to furnish stimulus to intellectual growth and culture.[29]

The author wanted to emphasize the social and civic aspects of the club over and above educational ones.

By 1930 the 59 active members usually met in private homes. "We feel the Club fills a much needed place in the lives of its members by reason of keeping them interested in affairs of the day, in art, music, drama. It gives them an opportunity which is usually given to men only, of keeping alert."[30] At about the same time, the club initiated a few changes to its constitution and bylaws. The most significant one was to omit the word "young" from Article III. Youth was no longer a requirement for membership.

In the fall of 1933, San José was in shock over the kidnapping of the young and handsome heir to the Hart Department Store business. The 21-year-old had recently graduated from Santa Clara College, was enormously popular, and was working toward taking over the family's retail enterprises. The minutes from the To Kalon meeting shortly after the kidnapping indicate that the club sent "a note of sympathy to the Hart family."[31] Two weeks later, after the body of Brooke Hart had been discovered and the accused kidnappers lynched in Saint James Park, the tone expressed in To Kalon Club minutes is decidedly stronger. It reads:

> Believing that the inefficiency of our criminal laws and the laxity of their enforcement has resulted in the breakdown of the respect for all laws, we, the members of To Kalon desire to go on record as favoring any constructive effort to so reform the criminal laws of California that the prosecution of criminals may be made more effective.[32]

The club has not formally petitioned the government to change criminal law since.

Beginning in 1939, To Kalon sponsored an annual concert series at the San José Civic Auditorium featuring opera, chamber, and symphonic music. Over the next several

*The original group of Chapter DK P.E.O. The twelve were organized at Clara Edward's 13th St. home in San José, March 1924. Several were also To Kalon members. Top row, left to right: Effie Hunt, Iva Smith, Evelyn Rudolph, Muriel Rudolph, Hazel Hopkins, Maude Curtiss, Grace Herold. Lower row, left to right: Clara Edwards, Ivadell Bohnett, Cora Foster, Bernice Hill.*
Courtesy of Nancy Drew.

*U.S.O. Building near the City Hall building in Plaza Park (today's Plaza de César Chavez) in San José. This building was the site of many social events during the war years. To Kalon Club members did volunteer work here.*

Courtesy of History San José.

years, the club sponsored the appearance of Jascha Heifitz, Marian Anderson, Yehudi Menuhin, Lily Pons, the Ballet Russe, and the San Carlo Opera.

To Kalon members did a considerable amount of volunteer work at the USO hut, the hospitality house for servicemen during the Second World War in downtown San José. The modest, framed building was at the south end of Plaza Park, and had been built in one day by a cadre of volunteers. Even after the war, in February 1946, the minutes itemize what club members donated and served to over five hundred servicemen. Five hundred sandwiches made by club members, were served to the "boys," who drank so much milk that water had to be substituted when the milk ran out. Besides the sandwiches, "four sheet cakes, twenty dozen small cakes, and eight dozen butterflies" were consumed.[33]

## Changing Traditions

Members had to be reminded in 1955 that "directors meetings are secret."[34] The directors accepted or rejected new members, and perhaps some of that conversation was made public. In 1958 a motion was considered to reduce the number of meetings from weekly to twice per month, but it did not win a two-thirds majority and was defeated. Twenty-five years later, in 1983, reducing the number of meetings to two per month won approval. In 1966 several changes were made to the bylaws, including "the custom of the tea table shall be discontinued at the discretion of the hostess or hostesses on such occasions as guest days or the President's Tea."[35]

**PRESIDENT'S TEA**—Pouring at the annual To Kalon tea Thursday are Mrs. Leah Watts, left, and Mrs. Robert M. Moore, the group's outgoing president. Standing, from left, are Mesdames Eugene R. Booker, Charles E. Luck-hardt, Curtis Lindsay, Adrien Lassere and Ralph W. Shafor, new To Kalon president for whom the tea was given. Setting for the affair was the Los Gatos home of Mrs. William Binder.

*Newspaper photograph of the "President's Tea," from a decidedly more formal era than today.*
Courtesy of the *San Jose Evening News*, October 4, 1957.

A page from To Kalon's scrapbook picturing many past presidents, 2001.

Marty Lion
(President)

Beryl Rodenbaugh and Carol Sheilds-
presenting roses as Program Chairs

# Past President's Tea 2001

Alice
Orth
(Pres.)

LaVerne
Schmidt
(Pres.)

Joanne
Petersen
(Pres.)

Millie McBrian  JoAnn Risko  Betty Kirtland
(Pres.)

Beryl
Rodenbaugh

Helen Moore
(Pres.)

Mary Collins
(Pres.)

Marjolie
Thomas

JoAnne
Hersch

Huette
James
(Pres.)

Lois
McDonald
(Pres.)

Ruth Guderian and Joan Scott (Pres.)
at Charlene Snells' home.

Up until about 1960, it was customary for club members to wear hats and gloves for meetings and events. At about that time, this expectation was relaxed, and those accessories made optional. Wearing pants to meetings was still severely frowned upon. Kathryn Walter recalled: "I remember Carol Luckhardt, Nancy Parton, and myself discussing 'could we wear *pantsuits* to the annual picnic in 1980?'" That would have been a first."[36] Evidently Dorothy Farrington, the acknowledged "grand dame" of the club, was the first to wear pants to a club meeting, astonishing the other members.

In 1978, the club celebrated the seventy-fifth anniversary of the establishment of To Kalon. The first meeting that fall, held at Barbara (Mrs. Hugh S.) Center's home, honored those members who had been in the club for fifty years or more. Azalea (Mrs. Earl) Alderman, Effie (Mrs. Harold) Hunt, Vi (Mrs. Eugene) Lawrence, and Lulu (Mrs. Benjamin) Ledyard, were given special corsages.

The membership was still a comfortable enclave of women who knew each other or each other's families. No one would have even considered suggesting the use of name tags. All of that was about to change with the loss of longtime members during the last decades of the twentieth century.

*Wilma Borchers (left), Helen Hall (center), and Dorothy Farrington, at the San José Country Club, 1982.*

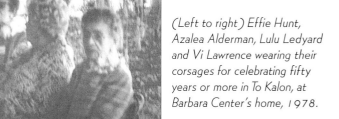

*(Left to right) Effie Hunt, Azalea Alderman, Lulu Ledyard and Vi Lawrence wearing their corsages for celebrating fifty years or more in To Kalon, at Barbara Center's home, 1978.*

YWC Ledger,
1903.
Reproduction courtesy
of History San José.

| 1903. | Dues | | Disbursements | |
|---|---|---|---|---|
| Oct. 8 | Generive Chambers | 2 00 | Oct. 22 1 yd. Black-board | 90 |
| " " | Helen Stocking | 2 00 | " " 1 Secretary's book | 75 |
| " 15 | Amy S. Blanchard | 2 00 | " " 1 Treasurer's book | 60 |
| " " | Ella Brady | 2 00 | | 2 25 |
| " " | Florence Granger | 2 00 | Oct. 31 By Balance | 23 75 |
| " " | Edith Granger | 2 00 | | |
| " " | Edith MacChesney | 2 00 | | |
| " " | Effie Pruhn | 2 00 | | |
| " 22 | May Morton | 2 00 | | |
| " " | Nellie Evans | 2 00 | | |
| " " | May Evans | 2 00 | | |
| " 29 | Nettie Dinsmore | 2 00 | | |
| | Maud S. Bailey | 2 00 | | |
| | | 26 00 | | 26 00 |
| Nov. 1 | Balance | 23 75 | Nov. 5 Room-Rent (for Oct) | 1 00 |
| " 3 | Dorothea Cain | 2 00 | " " Rollcall book ink | |
| " 5 | Etta W. Bailey | 2 00 | " " Chalk eraser | 40 |
| " 12 | Bertha Aras | 2 00 | " " Blackboard frame | 50 |
| " " | Ruby Brooks | 2 00 | " " Rent for Unitarian Parlors | 6 00 |
| | | 31 75 | " 12 Invitations | 2 00 |
| | | | Club Invitations | 2 00 |
| | | | Ideal Tea Stores | 80 |
| | | | Place Crockery | 1 85 |
| | | | Maid | 1 50 |
| | | | Red Paper | 10 |
| | | | Paper Napkins | 40 |
| | | | | 16 55 |
| | | | Nov 30 By Balance | 15 20 |
| | | | | 31 75 |
| Dec. 1 | Balance | 15 20 | | |
| Dec. 10 | Helen Ellis | 2 00 | Dec. 9 Room Rent (Nov & Dec) | 2 00 |
| " " | Edith Stahl | 2 00 | | |
| " " | Georgine Bean | 2 00 | Dec. 31 By Balance | 27 20 |
| " " | Florence Latta | 2 00 | | |
| " " | Edna Latta | 2 00 | | |
| " 17 | Georgie Willey | 2 00 | | |
| " " | Stella Pruhn | 2 00 | | |
| | | 29 20 | | 29 20 |

# CHAPTER THREE

## *Financial Report*

WHEN THE **YWC** BEGAN MEETING IN **1903,** many of the young women would have paid a nickel to ride the street car to the meeting. The dress they were wearing could have been purchased at Hart's Department Store or The Arcade for about $20, and their lace-up, two-inch heeled leather shoes sold for $3 at Herold's Shoe Store on Santa Clara Street. Glancing at the advertisements in the San José *Mercury Herald* that year gives us an idea of the local cost of living. A six-room, Naglee Park cottage was listed for $3,000. Fruit ranch land sold for $150 an acre, and 160 acres in the hills above Los Gatos was listed for $8,200.[37]

The YWC's first ledger is set up in a very simple manner: the left column labeled "Dues" (for income), and the right column labeled "Disbursements." Maud (Mrs. Gilchrist) Bailey was the first treasurer, and her neat cursive lists the dues-paying members and the various expenses of that first year. Necessary items included the secretary's book for $.75 and the treasurer's book for $.60. The club purchased a copy of *Shattuck's Rules* for $.75 as a reference for parliamentary procedure. It also procured a blackboard, chalk and erasers for $1.80.

The only source of income was dues. Each member paid $2 in dues for the year.

"From the beginning, the most basic cost charged to the club was a room rental fee."

Christmastime in front of Hart's Department Store in San José, 1925.
Courtesy of History San José.

By 1908 there was also a $1 initiation fee. After the club changed its name to To Kalon in 1918, dues were $2.50 per year with a $3.00 initiation fee. By the time To Kalon was twenty-five years old, dues were $10 annually with a $5 initiation fee. During World War II, there was a motion to raise the initiation fee to $15, but members voted against the proposal. By To Kalon's 50th birthday in 1953, annual dues were $17 and the initiation fee had jumped to $25. As of To Kalon's 100th birthday, the initiation fee is $65, and dues are $75 per year.

*Fred Brohaska's Orchestra, which performed at many San José events, including for the To Kalon Club.*
Courtesy of History San José.

In 1907 a woman dishwasher cost the club $.70 for an event, and the club paid a fortune teller $3.50. A 1912 luncheon at the Vendome Hotel cost $1.25 per person. Each member paid $1, and the club treasury contributed $.25 per person. In 1913, a Mrs. Wilcox was paid $.60 for cakes, and the next year, local orchestra leader Fred Brohaska was paid $8.

From the beginning, the most basic cost charged to the club was a room rental fee. In 1903, the YWC paid $1 per month for use of a room in the Porter Building, plus the cost of coal for heating. That cost remained static until after the 1906 earthquake when the club began using the San José Woman's Clubhouse, paying $1 per month for it. The YWC appears to have fallen behind in rent payments, since in May 1913 it owed the woman's club $12 in back rent, which it gave its approval to pay. Perhaps this could have contributed to a conflict resulting in the parting of the ways between the two clubs. In 1914, the YWC gave

$20 toward the building fund for the new Young Woman's Christian Association (YWCA) building, and when it was completed two years later, it began to hold its meetings there. The club paid $2.50 per month rent to the YWCA.[38]

Like many women's clubs, the YWC desired its own clubhouse to meet and carry on business. For the first decade, when the club identified itself as

*San José Woman's Clubhouse, 2002.*
Photograph by the author.

an auxiliary to the San José Woman's Club, the young women participated in fundraisers to accumulate money for a San José Woman's Clubhouse. In 1906 after raising $4,000, the woman's club bought and occupied the former Leddy home, a rambling eleven-room frame house at 43 South Third Street, and the young women were allowed the use of a meeting room there. The woman's club used that building until the 1920s when it acquired property at 75 South Eleventh Street and built a mission-style clubhouse. It is still in use today, and is designated a historic landmark by the City of San José.

As the younger women grew older, however, they mapped out a future independent of the San José Woman's Club. By 1918, when the YWC became known as the To Kalon Club, it established a fund to save for a To Kalon clubhouse. The account grew modestly through the 1920s, and by 1932 had almost $700. Unfortunately, the club's banker, California Mutual Building & Loan Association, filed for bankruptcy in 1932, like many other financial institutions caught in the Great Depression. To Kalon had to file a claim against the bank, and a few years later, recovered some liquidating dividends, but they never amounted to the original loss. Since then, To Kalon has not pursued owning a clubhouse.

Another expense incurred by the club was printing its annual agenda. It emulated most women's clubs across the country and went to great effort and expense to have club material printed. One historian has pointed out that "by printing a yearlong program detailing topics and presenters, clubwomen provided evidence of their capacity for sustained and structured work."[39]

Oftentimes, clubs also printed documents like constitutions and bylaws, yearbooks, schedules, or memorials. For the first few years, the YWC spent between $5 and $12 per year to print programs. By the end of the 1920s, printing costs were about $45 per year. Today, those original programs are the most valuable primary source that we have to detail the week to week activities of the club in the early days.

Since the club had transformed itself in the 1920s, and members had quit making the presentations themselves, the biggest expense by far was the cost of presenters, musicians, or speakers. Late in the 1920s, costs for speakers, floral bouquets, and musicians were $425.[40] In 1942-43 the club spent almost $500 on speakers or artists, and ten years later, it had more than doubled to over $1,000. By the late 1950s, talent agent Betty Hutchens lined up speakers and artists for club programs, whose prices ranged from $50 to $80 per engagement.[41] Even though the club relegated the task of commissioning speakers to a talent agent, the cost of luncheon was still relatively modest. For example, the guest day luncheon at the Hotel Sainte Claire in 1959 still only cost $2.07 per person.

## Philanthropy

The club was often asked for charitable contributions. Some of the donations indicate the kind of projects supported by the members. In 1909, for example, the YWC gave $6 for the children's room at the library. In 1913 it contributed $5 toward the purchase of "the gore lot at the junction of First and Market streets."[42] The triangular little lot was intended as a new park. In 1915, the club gave $5 to the National Child Labor Commission and another $5 "for the Movement of the Unemployed."[43] During World War I, the club made donations to Belgian Relief, Armenian Relief, Jewish Relief, and the Red Cross. In 1917 a very successful pageant put on in San José to benefit the Red Cross featured almost 1,500 performers and attracted over five thousand people. The script was written by YWC member, Helen (Miss) Stocking.[44]

Each year, the YWC held a Christmas sewing bee, where members made doll clothing and dressed dolls for the children at the Home for Benevolence, "lovely enough to rejoice the heart of any small girl."[45] In 1915 it was at the home of Azalea (Mrs. Earl) Alderman who lived at Fifteenth and San Fernando streets. She also entertained her sewing guests with a harp solo. The Home for Benevolence was one of the beneficiaries of the good deeds of the YWC. It was San José's first orphanage, located at Martha and Eleventh streets, operated by the Ladies Benevolent Society, a woman's philanthropic group. Later, in the 1950s, it changed locations and names to the Eastfield Children's Home. In 1987, Eastfield merged with Ming Quong, a San Francisco-based protection home for Chinese girls, associated with the Presbyterian Church. Today, Eastfield Ming Quong, no longer an orphanage, offers mental health services and drug and alcohol education programs.

During the club year 1947-48, members engaged in considerable discussion about the role of To Kalon in charitable giving. The result was an addition to club bylaws:

> Because club dues are estimated and levied upon members to an amount sufficient only to defray the cost of programs and incidental expenses for the club year, and because members give individually to worthy causes, a further levy is therefore a duplication of gifts. It is the policy of the club not to donate as a unit to outside projects.[46]

Philanthropic contributions have remained modest because club members have been active on other boards of directors and support other causes. Symbolic donations have been made by the club to the San José Symphony, History San José, San José Museum of Art, the San José/Cleveland Ballet, Ainsley House Heritage Campaign, Council of Churches Food Closet, and Timpany Center. Fundraising has never been a goal of the To Kalon Club.

One of the reasons that To Kalon has limited its commitment to fundraising and charitable giving is because many members make substantial private contributions to charitable causes. Indeed a number of members have given the community historic buildings, educational facilities, and community centers. To Kalon member Helen Timpany and her husband, Charles, were the benefactors of, among many other causes, the Timpany Center. It is a therapeutic center for the disabled, emphasizing aquatics. The pool there enables many who would otherwise not have access to swimming to experience high-level physical therapy.

Phyllis Simpkins and her husband, Alan, have been generous supporters of her Alma Mater, San José State University. They have funded the Simpkins Athletic Center and the administrative building for the athletic department at the university. Both the Simpkins were awarded honorary doctorates from the university, and the prestigious Tower Award, for their "longstanding pattern of generosity."

*Frances Fox (left) and Helen Timpany, Calvary Methodist Church, 1993.*

*Phyllis Simpkins, at History San José.*

*Gerry Hicks (left),
Soo Krogstad, and
Susan Anderson, Guest Day
Tea, 2001.*

To Kalon member Gerry Hicks was instrumental in donating the English Tudor-styled Ainsley House, her Lloyd family home, to the City of Campbell. It was built in 1925 at Hamilton and Bascom avenues, and it was moved to its present location in downtown Campbell in 1990. Its fifteen rooms have been carefully restored and it houses the Campbell Historical Museum. The surrounding English gardens and grounds are used for weddings and other community functions.

*Ainsley House,
donated to the City
of Campbell by
club member
Gerry Hicks.*

Photograph courtesy of
Heritage Council of Santa
Clara County.

Likewise, club member Lois Brown's family donated the Jamison Brown House to the City of Santa Clara, located near the Triton Museum of Art in Santa Clara. It had been at her family's pear orchard, and the house was moved to its present location in the 1980s. The historic house can be rented for meetings and gatherings.

The Kirk-Farrington House is the headquarters for the San José Junior League and the Farrington Historical Foundation. It was the family home of club member Dorothy Farrington's husband. She bequeathed the property and its contents to the foundation, and today it is an historic home and garden, and the site of many community functions.

These historic buildings and community contributions highlight the traditional generosity of club members, even though the club itself does not take on major fundraising projects. Some club members have also made financial and personal commitments to the community, but not in a public forum. The "Roll Call" of members can illuminate the individuals who have made up the club over the years, and the roles that they have played in their families and in their communities.

*Jamison-Brown House, Santa Clara, 2002. This house was home to club member Lois Brown's family, and was donated an moved to its present site near the Triton Museum in Santa Clara. Author Jack London purportedly wrote his famous book* The Call of the Wild *on the veranda of this house.*

Photograph by Patrick M. Ignoffo.

*Kirk-Farrington House, 2002. This home was built in the nineteenth century by Theophilus Kirk. Two of his children, Ethel and Edith Kirk, were charter members of the Young Woman's Club in 1902. The house was inherited by Edith's son, Theo Kirk Farrington and his wife, Dorothy (Bogen) Farrington. she was a longtime member of to Kalon, and many club events have been held here.*

Photograph by Patrick M. Ignoffo.

46

October 7. 1943

| | Oct. 7 | Oct. 14 | Oct. 21 | Oct. 28 | Nov. 11 | Nov. 18 | Nov. 25 | Dec. 2 | Dec. 9 | 1944 | January 17 | Jan. 20 | Jan. 27 | Feb. 3 | Feb. 10 | Feb. 17 | Feb. 24 | Mar. 2 | Mar. 9 | Mar. 16 | Mar. 23 | Mar. 30 | Apr. 6 |
|---|---|---|---|---|---|---|---|---|---|---|---|---|---|---|---|---|---|---|---|---|---|---|---|
| Alderman Mrs Earl P. | x | x | | | x | x | x | x | x | | | excused | - | - | - | - | - | - | - | - | - | - | - |
| Atkinson Mrs W Leroy | a | x | | a | x | x a a | | | | | | a | x | x | x | a | | | | | | | |
| Blanchard Mrs Oliss | x | x | x | x | a | x | | | | | | a | x | x | | x | | | | | | | |
| Bohnett " L. D. | x | x | x | x | a | x | x | | | | | a | x | a | x | x | a | | | | | | |
| Braslan " Charles P. | x | x | x | x | a x a | a | | | | | | a | x | a | a a | a | x | | | | | | |
| Bullock " Newell H. | x | a | a | a | a a x | x | | | | | | a | x a | a a a x a a | | | | | | | | |
| Burchfiel " Cecil M. | a | a | a | x | x x x | a | | | | | | a | x | a x x x x a | | | | | | | | |
| Butcher " Arthur | a | x | x | x | x x a | | | | | | | a | a a a a a a a a a | | | | | | | | |
| Campbell " Frank P. | x | a | a | x | a a a | a | | | | | | a | a a a x a | | | | | | | | |
| Call " Delmar | x | a | x | x | x x a | | | | | | | a | x x x x | a | | | | | | | |
| Chase " S. Harold | x | a | a | a | x a x a | a | | | | | | a | x x x x | a | | | | | | | |
| Crider " J Walter | x | a | a | a | x a x a | | | | | | | a | x a | a | x | | | | | | | |
| Curtiss " Frederick | x | x | x | x | a x x a | a | | | | | | a | x a | x | a a | | | | | | | |
| Dahleen " Henry | x | x | x | a | x x a | | | | | | | x | x | x x | x | | | | | | | |
| Donovan Miss Dorothy | x | x | x | x | x x x | x | | | | | | x | x x x a a | | | | | | | | |
| Dorn Mrs Henry | x | x | x | x | a a x | a | | | | | | x | x | a | a a a | | | | | | | |
| Edwards " Leonard R. | x | a | x | x | a a x | a | | | | | | x a | x | x a | a | | | | | | | |
| Free " Arthur M. | a | x | x | x | a a x | x | | | | | | a | x | x | x a | | | | | | | |
| Garner " Clarence M. | x | a a | x | x | a x a | | | | | | | x | x | x | a a | a a | | | | | | |
| Gledding " A. L. | x | a | x | x | a a | a | | | | | | x | x | x | x | x | | | | | | |
| Gluektich Miss Kathryne | | | | | | | | | | | | | x x x x a | | | | | | | | |
| Harlan Miss Minnie J. | a | x | x | a | x a x | x | | | | | | a x | x x a | a | x | | | | | | |
| Haynard " F Roy | a | a | x | a | x a a | | | | | | | x | x | x | a | a | | | | | | |
| Herold " Harvey | x | x | x | x | a x x a | a | | | | | | x | x | x | a a | x | | | | | | |
| Hill " Henrie | x | a | x | x | a x x | a | | | | | | a | x | a a | x x | | | | | | | |
| Hines " A. D. | a | a | a | a | a x x | a | | | | | | - | - | - | - | - | - | - | - | - | - | - | - |
| Hopkins " Mark F. | | | | | | | | | | | | | x x x x a | | | | | | | | |
| Hunt " G. Walter | -Associate- | | | | | | | | | | | | | | | | | | | | | | |
| Hunt " Harold G. | x | x | x | x | x x x | x | | | | | | x | a x | x a | a | x | | | | | | |
| Husted " J. R. | x | x | x | x | a x x a a | | | | | | | a | a a a a x a a | | | | | | | | |
| Jones " Elizabeth Ann | x | a | a | x | x a x a a | | | | | | | | | | | | | | | | | |

Attendance record,
1943.

44

# Chapter Four

## Roll Call

The faded and brittle pages in one of To Kalon's small, leather-bound attendance books read like a litany belonging in a San José history. Familiar names leap off the pages, conjuring characters from Santa Clara Valley's past. At the beginning the membership was made up of the daughters and friends of members of the San José Woman's Club. The fathers of the young women were professionals or merchants in San José. All were caucasian, solidly middle class, or rising to upper class. At the turn of the century, San José had only a handful of truly wealthy families. Edith MacChesney's father was a physician, Maud McClish's father was the president of College of the Pacific, Florence and Edna Latta's father was an orchardist, and Marguerite Dinsmore's father was a clergyman. The Kirk sisters' father had devised a plan to irrigate orchards and had a thriving business implementing his designs.

A typical characteristic of women's clubs across the country was that memberships were comprised of networks of relations. Mothers would invite daughters and daughters-in-law, sisters would invite their husband's sisters or mothers. Club memberships tightened already close-knit communities.

Several sets of sisters joined the YWC as charter members. Ethel Kirk and her sister, Edith, joined in 1903. Their father, Theophilus Kirk, was an orchardist who

> "Club memberships tightened already close-knit communities."

organized the Kirk Ditch Company, an irrigation company which ran irrigation lines through hundreds of Santa Clara Valley orchards. He was extremely successful, and he built a show-place Victorian home on Dry Creek Road. Edith married J. P. Dorrance, and Ethel married S. D. Farrington. Ethel's son, Theo Kirk Farrington, married Dorothy Bogen, who would also become an important member of To Kalon for many years.

Dorothy (Mrs. Theo) Farrington was somewhat eccentric and outspoken, and was described by member Huette James as "a maverick, but also the grand dame."[47] She owned several homes, including one in Pacific Grove, another in Lake Tahoe, and a flat in San Francisco, and she enjoyed cruising around town in her English taxicab. She had an extensive collection of couture clothing and over four hundred hats. Dorothy bequeathed the Victorian that Edith and Ethel Kirk had been raised in, and all its contents, to the Farrington Historical Foundation.

Another set of sisters with charter membership dating from 1903 were Edna Latta and her sister, Florence. They lived on North Third Street, and their father was an orchardist. Edna served as corresponding secretary in the early years, and from 1922-1924 and was To Kalon's treasurer. She never married, and was an active club member for almost sixty years, becoming an honorary member in 1960.

The Granger sisters, Edith and Florence, lived on South Tenth Street and were the daughters of F. S. Granger, the general manager of the San José and Los Gatos railroad. Sixty years later, Florence Granger was still associated with the club. Edith and Katherine Stahl were both students, Edith attending Stanford University. The family lived just off Saint James Park. Their mother was a proofreader for the *Mercury Herald* and their father the proprietor of Putnam & Stahl, a real estate, insurance, loans, and collections business at 34 W. Santa Clara Street.

Several families were represented in To Kalon in multiple generations. One of the forty-eight charter members was Maud (Mrs. Leo) Archer. The Archers were an old San José family who lived at the Vendome Hotel, and Leo was a prominent San José attorney. During the same era, Mrs. Hugh Center was an active member of the San José Woman's Club. Her son, Hugh Stuart Center, eventually married the Archers' daughter, Jane. To Kalon member Marion Langley remembers attending the couple's bridal shower in Archer's home, the penthouse of the De Anza Hotel. "Mrs. Archer liked gardening and she installed a beautiful rooftop garden from which one could see the entire valley."[48] Jane died early, and Hugh's second wife, Barbara, joined To Kalon. Today, the Hugh Stuart Center Charitable Trust supports several organizations, and has funded this anniversary publication.

*Doris Drennan (left), Marion Langley (center), and Beth Lindsay at the annual meeting at the Chinchen home, 1990.*

Marion Langley's mother was Charlotte (Mrs. William LeRoy "Roy") Atkinson, who joined in 1921. "Although I was little, I looked forward to Wednesday and Thursday nights at the dinner table. My mother and father would recount the speakers from their clubs. On Wednesday we had Rotary for dinner and on Thursday, To Kalon. As children, my sisters and I learned a lot at the dinner table."[49] Mrs. Atkinson's family, the Brays, had a home called "Roseland" near today's El Camino Real and Scott Boulevard in Santa Clara. "W .L." Atkinson, as he was called, was a prominent realtor and civic leader, serving on San José City Council and the San José Water District, and in a variety of other capacities.

Women in the Schoenheit-Moore family have been club members for ninety-five

*Winifred Schoenheit (left) and Evelyn Rudolph at the home of Zura Lindsay, 1959.*

*Mary Frances Wines (left) and Helen Moore, at the San Jose Country Club, 1999*

of the past one hundred years. Winifred (Mrs. Augustus A.) Schoenheit joined in 1908, and in 1910 was treasurer. Her husband had followed in his father's footsteps as a druggist in San José, but sold the business in 1907. He went to work for the Security State Bank and later purchased a thirty-six acre ranch on Stevens Creek Road where his family resided. Winifred was still a member in 1960-61. Her daughter, the late Helen (Mrs. Robert) Moore, and her granddaughter-in-law, Julie (Mrs. Douglas) Moore, were long-time members of the club. Helen claimed she was the "last leaf on the tree" of her generation. Reiterating what Marion Langley reported about club news, "Every Thursday my father and I would sit at the dinner table and hear what went on that day at To Kalon."[50]

Helen (Mrs. Richard) Moore may have been an unwitting beneficiary of To Kalon's emphasis on intellectual growth. She attended Stanford University, earning her degree in 1926. She joined To Kalon in 1936, served as president in 1956 and spent several years on the board of directors. She recalled, "We had wonderful programs. Early San José didn't have anything for women to do outside of the home."[51]

Cora (Mrs. Albert) Foster and her husband had an orchard on Capital Avenue and he was the county agricultural commissioner. She was a watercolor artist and sold some of her work to Gumps, the exclusive San Francisco store. Her daughter, Betty (Mrs. Richard) Wells, inherited her artistic bent, and she taught art, flower arrangement, and interior design at San José State. And for several years after teaching, she had her own interior design business. She joined the club herself in 1948.

Betty recalled being a young child when her mother hosted a To Kalon meeting at their Capital Avenue home in 1922. Her mother asked her to turn the cuckoo clock off so it would not disturb the meeting. "At that time, Capital Avenue was just a two-lane dirt road leading to Alum Rock Park," and young Betty waited in the front yard for the guests to arrive. While the program was on, Betty played in the front yard. A curious neighbor driving by stopped to gape at all the cars parked there. She laughed when she recalled that he asked, "What's the matter, Betty? Did somebody die?"[52] Evidently the neighbor could not imagine why so many cars would be at the house.

The children of the first generation of club members were keenly aware of their mothers' participation in club activities. It influenced their own educational aspirations, many seeking college education. The children heard all the club topics at their own family dinner table. And finally, many daughters of these early members became members themselves and passed on club interest to their own daughters.

The merchant community was also strongly represented in To Kalon. Zura (Mrs. Curtis) Lindsay joined the club in 1928. She and her husband, Curtis, had come to San José in 1925, and opened a stationery and office supplies store at 77 South First Street. He was active in the downtown merchant community, and when he died in 1958, Zura took over as president of Curtis Lindsay, Incorporated. She was active in To Kalon until

*Betty Wells (left), Ruth Nicholson (center), and Patty Twist, at the San José Country Club, 1987.*

she died in 1978. Her daughter-in-law, Beth (Mrs. Wesley) Lindsay, joined in 1956 and served as president nine years later.

Marie (Mrs. Edmund N.) Richmond's husband was the proprietor of one of the largest fruit canneries in the Santa Clara Valley. Incorporated in 1919, the Richmond-Chase Company remained a powerful economic force in the fruit industry of the Santa Clara Valley well into the 1950s. Edmund belonged to the prestigious Sainte Claire Club, and Marie served as president of the To Kalon Club in 1937. Her daughter-in-law, Helen (Mrs. Burnell E.) Richmond, also was a member and president of To Kalon.

Mabel (Mrs. Arthur) Free was the wife of a five-term Republican Congressman. She and her husband had spent the early years of their marriage in Mountain View, where he was that town's first city attorney. They moved their five children, including two sets of twins, to San José when he became district attorney, and in 1921 he was elected to Congress. According to one source, "Mrs. Free enjoyed a brilliant social career during their 12 years in the Capitol City. The Frees were frequently guests at the famous State House dinners and met many of the leading foreign celebrities of the day."[53] An avid golfer, she was active in To Kalon for many years.

Barbara Center (left) and Patty Oneal, at the Blair home, 1979.

Patty (Mrs. Duncan) Oneal joined the club in 1948. Born in Gilroy, she attended U.C. Berkeley, earned a bachelor's degree and teaching credential from San José State, and became a kindergarten teacher. In 1930 she married Duncan Oneal, the only son of Anna and Louis Oneal of San José. The press dubbed Louis a "self-made baron of the old west"[54] because he loved to entertain on his O & O horse ranch in the Los Altos Hills. He hobnobbed with state and local political leaders and exerted great influence in San José politics. His law firm was the most prestigious in town.

His son, Duncan, earned a law degree at Stanford and joined his law firm located in the First National Bank building. His wife, Patty, joined To Kalon, and took to the club immediately, becoming its president within two years. In 1969 Patty invited her daughter-in-law, Shirley Oneal, to join the club. "I was young, and for To Kalon, quite young. Most of the other members were my mother-in-law's age. They thought they should get some younger women into the club if it was to keep going. So they looked to their daughters and daughters-in-law."[55] Shirley's sister-in-law, Mimi (Mrs. Dan) Oneal, joined in 1990. Both Mimi and Shirley have had leadership roles in the club.

The Crummey family was important to San José's history as well as to To Kalon. The Crummeys lived next door to the Schoenheits on North Fifth Street. John Crummey was a devout Methodist, who never took a drink and taught Sunday school. His daughter, Beth (Mrs. Arthur) Chinchen recalled, "Our whole life was tied up in church. I never had to think of what I was going to do—everything was church. Even youth outings and field trips."[56]

John Crummey was the grandson of inventor John Bean, who revolutionized insecticide spraying of orchard fruit. Crummey capitalized on his grandfather's invention to launch Food Machinery Corporation, producing automated food processing and cannery equipment. During and after World War II, Food Machinery evolved into a major producer of military tanks and other defense equipment. Today the company is known simply as FMC.

Daughters Beth and Faith attended the College of the Pacific while it was in San José. When the college relocated to Stockton, Faith went there and earned her degree in

*Shirley Oneal (seated),
Marty Lion (center), and
Charlene Snell, Fall Tea, 1998,
at Marty Lion's home.*

*Joanne Peterson (left) and
Mimi Oneal, Summer Picnic,
1998, at Beth Chinchen's home.*

Caren Hebeler (left), Caroline Crummey (center) and Beth Chinchen, three generations of the Crummey and Chinchen families, 1996.

1923. Club member Beth (Mrs. Arthur) Chinchen explained that she never considered herself club material. She recalled, "I was never part of society. We were farmers."[57] Beth and her husband, Arthur, owned pear orchards in today's Rose Garden neighborhood off University Avenue. They also operated two packinghouses. She added that she "would never have joined something that took that much time [To Kalon] when my husband was alive."[58]

Nevertheless, Beth, her sisters Faith (Mrs. Paul) Davies and Marie (Mrs. Robert) Foster, and her father's second wife, Caroline, all became active members of the club. Later, her daughter-in-law, Diane (Mrs. Stanley) Chinchen, and her granddaughter, Caren (Mrs. Christopher) Hebeler, also joined. At one

Phyllis Simpkins (left), Joan Scott (center), and Beth Chinchen, celebrating Beth's 100th birthday, 2002.

time, this family had four generations represented as members of To Kalon: Caroline Crummey, Beth Chinchen, Diane Chinchen, and Caren Hebeler. Beth Chinchen was a cherished To Kalon member, and in 2002, when the Christopher Barbershop Quartet performed for the club, they sang a special song to her which, as Gerry Hicks noted, "brought a lump to everyone's throat."[59] Beth Chinchen celebrated her centennial birthday in May 2002, and she died just three months later.

Huette (Mrs. Robert) James was the daughter-in-law of Elmerna (Mrs. Henry) Down and the niece of Alice (Mrs. Charles) Luckhardt. Alice's daughter-in-law, Carol (Mrs. John) Luckhardt, joined in 1974. She reported that, "When my mother-in-law entertained To Kalon at their home, she would have her two young sons pass cream and sugar, nuts and mints. According to my husband (John Luckhardt), the ladies loved the two little boys helping in this way. He kiddingly remarks, today, that when he retires he'd like to 'join' To Kalon!"[60]

Wilna (Mrs. Floyd) Parton's two daughters-in-law, Jackie and Nancy, were also members of the club. Nancy served as president in 1989-90.

Each Thursday, after the minutes were read and the finances reported upon, roll was called. Attendance was a strict requirement. After four unexcused absences the offender would be asked to resign.[61] The fragile, old record books have a careful and precise handwritten list of each year's membership. Narrow, straight columns extend across the page from each name, with an entry for every meeting of the year. An 'x' indicated the member was present and an 'a' constituted absence. A notation was made if the absence was excused.

Many members sought a formal leave of absence for an extended vacation, a serious illness, or the birth of a child. Much later, during World War II when gasoline was rationed, a number of members living in outlying areas of the Santa Clara Valley were unable to travel To Kalon meetings. During those years, normal protocol was reversed, and members were requested to notify the hostess when they *could* come to a meeting. All others were excused.

Carol Luckhardt (left) and Julie Moore, Calvary Methodist Church, 1994.

Lonna Franklin (left) and Nancy Parton at Filoli, 1998.

*Ruth Guderian (left) and Beryl Rodenbaugh, 2000.*

After 1907, the membership needed to be replenished as some drifted or moved away. The bylaws call for a member to put forward a nomination, two others must vouch for her, and her admittance was voted upon by directors. It was not simply a rubber stamp, and in at least one case in the 1930s, after a name had been presented, it was withdrawn because "she is not well known to many of our members."[62]

By the time the club became known as To Kalon in 1918, half of its members were married, and their husbands played important roles in the local economy. Halfway through the twentieth century, To Kalon was made up of the wives or relations of San José's political, social, and civic leaders. Today the club roster has older members than before, who come from a broader cross section of the Santa Clara Valley.

*Millie McBrian (left) and Joanne Skillicorn, at the San Jose Country Club, 2000*

*Carol Luckhardt (left), Colleen Lund (center), and Karen Shirey, 1999.*

*Sue Casey (left) and Margaret McNelly, 1999.*

*Betty Roberts and
Doris Drennan*

*A gathering of past presidents of To Kalon at Beth Chinchen's home.*

*Mary Collins, Mary Frances Wines, Elizabeth Jung
and Betty Kirtland.*

*Nancy Short (left) and Nancy Drew,
2002.*

*Marion Langley (left) and
Betty Bocks, 2000.*

## TO KALON

**1960**    **1961**

*To Kalon*

### PROGRAM

#### OCTOBER

✓ 13th—12:30 - - - - - Luncheon "Get-together"
     Program 2:30 - - by the Committee
    Mrs. E. Victor McDonald ✓ Mrs. Duncan Onea[...]
       1605 Emory, San Jose

✓ 20th—The Washington Scene - - - John Met[...]
      Mrs. Wesley Lindsay ✓
   10710 Ridgeview Avenue, San Jose

✓ 27th—My Work in Faraway Places - Robert W[...]
      Mrs. Lillian Roberts ✓
     Calvary Methodist Church,
    Naglee and Morse, San Jose

#### NOVEMBER

✓ 3rd—Twenty-four Women on a Mission t[...]
         Mrs. J[...]

     Mrs. Richard G. Wells ✓
    435 South 14th S[...]

10th—Africa To[...]
     Mr[...]
    Ca[...]

✓ 17th—Guest Da[...]
     Carme[...]
  Mrs. A. A. Sch[...]
     Calv[...]

✓ 1st—Life and Cust[...]
     Mrs[...]
   1845 Dr[...]

✓ 8th—Books to Lov[...]
     Mrs[...]
   1175 Univ[...]

✓ 15th—Holiday Hum[...]
     Mrs[...]
   5336 Gree[...]

Mrs. Paul F. Bo[...]
Calvary Methodist Church

[...]n to be announced
Mrs. James W. Lively ✓
264 Chula Vista, San Jos[...]

### MARCH

Students from Foreig[...]
Mrs. David Atkinson [...]
0 Canon Vista, San J[...]

[...]le - - - - - -
Mrs. Leah G. Watts
[...]vary Methodist Chu[...]

---

*To Kalon*

Please make these changes
in your calendar:

April 13 — Mrs. Bert Schroeder
  Town Club, Ste. Claire Hotel
  Speaker Robert Lindemann
  San Francisco jewel designer

April 27 — Mrs. Ralph Shafer
  Calvary Methodist church

May 4 — Mrs. Charles Luckhardt
  Calvary Methodist Church

May 18 — Picnic luncheon 12:30
  Mrs. John Bohnett
  [...] John Bohnett

# CHAPTER FIVE

# *Programs*

IN A RECENT SURVEY OF TO KALON MEMBERS, the single most important reason for main-taining membership was the consistent high quality of the programs. The breadth of interest reflected in the programs is the club's most distinguishing characteristic, has sus-tained its members and kept them coming back, and is what sets this club apart from oth-ers. A desire for education, thirst for cultural exchange, and love of learning is reflected in the lists of the hundreds of presenters to this club. To Kalon has heard poets and engi-neers, priests and rabbis, and scientists and interior designers speak on wide-ranging top-ics including travel, history and politics, art and interior design, and literature and music.

A program chair, with help from a committee, organizes programs for a coming club year. The monumental effort to organize speakers or presentations is embraced by the committee, and hugely appreciated by attendees. The result has been an honor roll of thought-provoking or inspirational presenters in whom the club can take great pride.

## Travel

Club members have been fascinated by travel, devoting at least one program each year to "Travel Talk." Occasionally travel formed the theme for an entire club year. In 1905-06, each program highlighted a different European capital, and the meetings became a

> "A diligent program chairwoman and committee is the key to strong programming..."

veritable travelogue as members or guests gave reports about the far-away cities. November and December focused on the United Kingdom, January and February on France, March and April on Italy. Celia (Mrs. Everett) Bailey noted that she "studied quite a bit on my paper," entitled "The Art Galleries of Rome," which she presented to the club on March 22, 1906.[63]

In the fall of 1910, the club explored Egypt in great detail. One popular guest speaker was a teacher from the State Normal School (San José State), Mrs. Mary George. The newspaper noted that her presentation was not a typical dry discussion of geographical facts, but that she spoke with a broader vision of "the geographical controls of the world and their influence over the lives, actions and aims of the people." Her descriptions of Egypt were "thrilling." "The desert seems to bring out the spiritual and the sublime," and "the view of the desert at sunset [is] the most glorious vision that earthly eyes can rest upon."[64]

The travel presentations began to take on a more personal touch when club members or guest speakers had actually been to the country that they were speaking about. The minutes from 1915 explain the use of a crude form of a slide projector to show travel images. "Miss Moore's talk was illustrated by the use of colored post cards which were thrown on the screen...."[65]

Alaska was a land of great mystery and adventure prior to the mid-twentieth century. To Kalon had a number of programs about Alaska, reflective of larger public interest in the vast, snowy territory in the far north. In 1919 guest speaker Mrs. Paul Clark's "Travel Talk"

*Diane Ferlotti,
Storyteller, 1991.*

was about Alaska. In the late 1920s and early 1930s, the club also welcomed the Jesuit priest Bernard Hubbard, S. J. to discuss his expeditions to Alaska. He earned the nickname of "the glacier priest" because of his repeated excursions into the Alaskan wilderness. He usually took young Santa Clara College men along with him, and they recorded his trips on still and movie film. The film footage remains among the only documentary film of that era in Alaska's history, and is held by the Smithsonian Institution in Washington, D.C.

Club members heard several programs dedicated to China over the years. In the spring of 1930, Dr. N. Wing Mah discussed "The Youth of China Today" at the home of Evelyn (Mrs. Paul) Rudolph. He elaborated "on Chinese history, past and present."[66] Two years later Mr. Ching Wah Lee spoke on "China's Cultural Heritage" and club members enjoyed lunch at Wings Yeun Fong Restaurant. In 1934, the Chinese Consul General Mr. K. W. Kwong gave another China-themed presentation. At this time, China was a U.S. ally.

*Katsuko Thielke, Teacher, at Hakone Gardens in Saratoga, 1991.*

There were programs on both Japan and India as well. In 1933, Mr. Shu Tomii, Consul General of Japan, spoke to the club. In 1925 Mrs. Paul Clark discussed her excursion to India, and after the war in January 1946, Mr. Sirdar Singh spoke about the "Renaissance in India."

To Kalon did not need to rely completely on outside experts for information about far away places. Its own members and their families traveled extensively, and were often willing to share their experiences with the club. Mr. and Mrs. John D. Crummey had gone to Africa in 1948. In November of that year, Mr. Crummey gave a presentation to To Kalon entitled, "Our Four Months in Africa." In 1952 he came before the club again to discuss "World Travel." Over the years, his three daughters and his second wife became members of the club.

## Performances

Musical and theatrical performances were important features of club meetings. Initially, club members would perform solos or duets, both vocals and instrumental. In 1912, Marian (Miss) Thompson sang several songs and was accompanied by Mrs. Dwight Ross on the piano. In 1922, at the Foster family home, Ruth (Mrs. L. D.) Bohnett played "Lullaby" from Jocelyn and "A Song Without Words," by Locke to entertain the club.

Occasionally the club hired performers to entertain. In 1915, Violinist Mary (Miss) Pasmore performed a musicale at the Vendome Hotel. She chose pieces by Tchaikovsky, Fritz Kreisler, and Eduard Napravnik to share with the club. The next year, club member Ida (Miss) Robson hosted *Madame Butterfly*, playing phonograph recordings of the entire opera. "Miss Robson has a fine Sonora phonograph and the records all by famous grand opera singers were much enjoyed."[67] Tea servers dressed in Japanese kimonos, lending dramatic effect to the afternoon. A notation in the minutes in 1915 says that "Mrs. Oliver Blanchard rendered two much appreciated whistling solos...."[68] Evidently the range of musical tastes for the YWC ran from formal opera to whistling a tune.

In 1916, Jennie Bacon gave a series of "humorous recitations." Bacon traveled the vaudeville circuit and was a talented comic actress. She and her husband, actor-play-wright Frank Bacon, had previously lived on a Mountain View ranch. After the San Francisco earthquake in 1906, the two moved to San José. Jennie managed a small, struggling theatre company at the José Theatre while her husband took parts in Oakland and San Francisco shows. In 1918, Frank Bacon finally had a Broadway hit with his play *Lightnin'*, in which he starred. Both the show and his acting ability got rave reviews and ran for a couple of years in New York.

To Kalon member Wilna (Mrs. Floyd) Parton was a talented musician, and provided music for many To Kalon events. At the New Year's party held in 1932 at the Hotel Sainte Claire, over 300 guests heard baritone Douglas Beattie perform, accompanied by Mrs. Parton. The duo included both classical arias in the program, as well as music composed by Californians.

Throughout the 1940s, the club hosted an annual concert series at the civic auditorium in San José. The club also had performances at its own meetings. Among the performances in this era was an April 1943 concert given by Yehudi Menuhin in San José where To Kalon members hosted a post-concert reception. In 1948, pianist Eva Garcia was a guest performer for the club at Wilna (Mrs. Floyd)

*Wilna Parton (bottom left) and Baritone Douglas Beattie (bottom right) from the "Society and Club Section" of the San Jose Mercury and Herald, January 3, 1932.*

**Concert Series Opens Tonight At Auditorium**

San Jose's Civic Auditorium will be ablaze with lights tonight for the opening performance of the 1946-47 concert series. Music lovers from all parts of the Valley as well as San Francisco and the Monterey Peninsula, will assemble this evening to hear Jan Peerce distinguished American tenor, inaugurate the 11th Annual Concert Series.

These splendid annual concerts have been sponsored since their inception 11 years ago by To Kalon Club, one of San Jose outstanding cultural organizations, and this season will be no exception. To Kalon is headed this year by Miss Dorothy Donovan, president of the group.

Jan Peerce is currently appearing with the San Francisco Opera Co. on the West Coast and the well known singer has won the highest praise from critics and musicians alike for his splendid performances in Verdi's "La Traviata" and "Rigoletto," and in Donizetti's "Lucia di Lammermoor." It will be remembered that Mr. Peerce made his local debut in the last named opera two years ago singing opposite Lily Pons.

Other outstanding artists to be brought here this year by Miss Denny and Miss Hazel Watrous of the Denny-Watrous Management will be Dorothy Maynor, Gregor Piatigorsky, Draper and Adler, Artur Rubinstein, Hurok's Ballet Russe de Monte Carlo, the Ballet de Monte Carlo, the Trudi Schoop Comic Ballet, the First Piano Quartet and the Los Angeles Philharmonic Orchestra.

Our thanks go to To Kalon and the Misses Denny and Watrous for sponsoring and making this series possible, since these artistic events have become an important cultural asset to the entire community.

Glimpsed above discussing San Jose's 11th Annual Concert Series which opens this evening at the Civic Auditorium are three members of To Kalon, Mesdames Floyd A. Parton, Curtis Morgan, Lindsay and Henry J. Down. To Kalon has sponsored these annual concerts this evening at the tion 11 years ago, thereby making an enormous contribution to the artistic and cultural life of the community. The world-famous American tenor, Jan Peerce, will inaugurate the season this evening and will be presented by the Denny-Watrous Management.

Parton's home in the eastern foothills. Choral groups have also entertained the club over the years, including the Monte Vista High School Impressions Choir, San José State Choraliers, and the Los Gatos Jazz Singers.

On the eve of World War II, the club heard a presentation from Bay Area radio anchor Arthur Linkletter. He had most recently been the radio announcer for the 1939 World's Fair at Treasure Island. His talk, "Ten Years in Show Business with Microphone and Aspirin," was a clever and humorous program. He went on to become a famous radio and television personality, author, and inspirational speaker.

At a 1989 club meeting, a local opera singer performed in Victorian style, as if she were singing at the Vendome Hotel at the turn of the twentieth century. To set the mood for the performance, she requested that the program chair, Mrs. Marion Langley, introduce the program as if she, too, were in Victorian-era San José. Although not given much time to prepare, Marion stepped into character to introduce, in extremely flowery language, the fictitious but "illustrious opera star, Miss Loretta Fitzwellen."[69]

## Current Events

In the early years, each meeting included a discussion of current events led by a member or someone from the San José Woman's Club. On many occasions, particular programs reflected the sentiment of national or international events. During World War I, for example, topics included food conservation, the Red Cross, and one program about two largely unknown technologies: "Aviation and the Submarine."[70] As World War I came to a close in 1919, "The New Geography of Europe" was presented by San José State professor, Mrs. Mary George, and "Italy After the War" was explained by Mr. Ettore

Patrizzi. In 1919, To Kalon purchased a $50 liberty bond and wrote letters to Senators James D. Phelan and Hiram Johnson endorsing the League of Nations.

Local and national politics shifted dramatically between the two world wars, and when the nation embraced President Franklin Roosevelt's New Deal, many Republicans were ousted from office. Five-term Republican Congressman Arthur Free, whose wife, Mabel, was a To Kalon member, presented a program in October 1934. "Mr. Arthur Free gave a very comprehensive talk on Socialism and Communism and on finishing explained the amendment to be voted on at the coming election."[71] Free lost the election, finishing off his lengthy political career.

In 1952, the club heard a presentation entitled "Kashmir—A Second Korea?" by W. G. Chattey and the following year on February 19, "Afghanistan: Her Peoples and Problems" by Clarita Rummel. It is eerie that To Kalon listened to those presentations fifty years ago, given the recent international focus on those regions.

Dr. Alfred G. Fisk presented "Formosa, Viet Nam and Nepal" in October 1957, long before most Americans could identify or locate Viet Nam. Dr. George Bruntz, a professor at San José State whose daughter-in-law, Sue, is a club member, spoke on contemporary issues facing the country on a number of occasions. Another professor, Dr. John R. Searle, spoke on January 22, 1970, on the topic, "Today's College Generation—How They Got That Way."

*Sue Bruntz (standing) with harpist Debbie Ricks, at Charlene Snell's home, 1999.*

## History and Politics

Local history has always intrigued To Kalon members—in part because many are descended from early San José settlers and residents. San José historian extraordinaire Clyde Arbuckle spoke on "Historical San José" in November, 1945. When Arbuckle died in 1998, it was estimated that over 40,000 people had heard his presentations on San José's history. His wife, Helen Arbuckle, a specialist on women in the history of the city, presented "San José Women" to club members in 1981. Other history presenters included Santa Clara University's history professor Father Henry Walsh, S.J. who spoke on "The History of Santa Clara Valley" in 1949, Santa Clara attorney Austen Warburton, who discussed California history, and author and Sunnyvale native Yvonne Jacobson, whose 1984 book, "*Passing Farms, Enduring Values*" recounts the orchard era of the valley.

To Kalon had a local history author within its own membership. Frances (Mrs. Theron) Fox, a Los Gatos native, authored, among other pieces, *Luís María Peralta and His Adobe* (1975) and she edited *Saratoga's First Hundred Years* by Florence R. Cunningham (1967). Her husband, Theron Fox, was also an historian. Frances was awarded San José *Mercury News* Woman of Achievement Award in both 1972 and 1974.

Neither the YWC nor To Kalon has ever been a strongly political organization. But at the beginning, the YWC supported some issues that were patently political even though they were never articulated that way. In 1903, the same year that the YWC was founded, Big Basin State Park was established in order to save the old growth redwoods of the Santa Cruz Mountains. Some of the most vocal supporters of the environmental

*Redwoods at Big Basin State Park, circa 1900.*

Courtesy of the Sourisseau Academy, San Jose State University.

save-the-redwoods groups were members of the San José Woman's Club and had daughters in the YWC, including Carrie Stevens Walter, the only woman on the official committee to establish the park. Later, just before World War I, there was a movement in California focused on Santa Clara County in particular, to regulate child labor, especially in canneries. The YWC wrote formal letters to government officials supporting Big Basin and requesting legislation to protect children. The club also made modest contributions to political causes such as Armenian relief and Belgian relief.

In the spring of 1917, Charles Parkinson, whose wife was a member, gave a presentation to the club urging the women to vote for a bond issue for new and improved county roads. He also brought the secretary of the chamber of commerce, Joseph Brooks, to campaign for passage of the bond issue. The New Year's Party that year had been at the Parkinson's home on The Alameda, but politics were left out. It was a strictly social card party for members and their husbands.

Although the club claimed to avoid political discussion, there have been politicians as presenters. California State Senator Herbert Jones, whose mother, Louise (Mrs. Stephen) Jones, had helped found the YWC, addressed "The Juvenile Question" in the fall of 1925. Jones's wife, (Mrs. Herbert) Jones, was also a member. During World War II, former Congressman Arthur Free shared "Letters From the Front," which described conditions faced by U.S. soldiers in battle. After the war in 1948, young Alan Cranston spoke to the club about the United Nations, a new international organization. Cranston went on to become a U.S. Senator from California.

*Betty Kirtland (left) and Ditty Smith, 1999, hosting the program "Lessons From Bosnia."*

Some local politicians, including San José mayors, have spoken to the club. And in 1998, San José State Political Science Professor Terry Christensen discussed local political power and California politics. Local civic leaders have also given presentations to the club, including long time San José City Manager, A. P. "Dutch" Hamann. His wife, Frances, was an active member of To Kalon, having been its president in 1972. Hamann was a somewhat controversial figure in San José history because he was ardently pro-growth, and his administration aggressively annexed tens of thousands of acres of farm land to the city. Frances and "Dutch" Hamann were both killed in an airline crash in the Canary Islands in 1977.

San José's Redevelopment Agency Director, Frank Taylor, also spoke to the club about civic issues in 1988. His vision for an economically robust downtown called for extremely aggressive policies on new developments. The following year, San José Police Chief Joseph McNamara came before the club. McNamara had gained national notoriety as a police chief-turned-detective writer, and he went on to become a fellow at the Hoover Institution at Stanford University. Laurie Smith, Sheriff of Santa Clara County spoke to the club in 2002. Secretary of Transportation in the Bush Administration, Norman Mineta was scheduled as the speaker for spring guest day in 2002. He cancelled his appearance, due in part to increased demand on his time from the September 11, 2001 attack on the World Trade Center in New York and the Pentagon in Washington, D.C.

## Literary

To Kalon members have demonstrated a decided interest in literature from the very beginning. In 1911, Laura (Miss) Bailey hosted an afternoon about Irish poetry, in which the newspaper reported that "her paper shows exhaustive study and yet the main points were presented in such a clear and scholarly manner that the listeners felt they had gained a better understanding of the history of Irish literature."[72] Selections were read from poets William Butler Yeats and Moira O'Neill. The presentation was held on Saint Patrick's Day, and tea and Irish treats were served after the program.

During the 1930s, local authors of some repute were guests of the club. In 1933 Kathleen Norris, author of eighty popular fiction books, discussed "The Road of the Writer." A reporter for the San Francisco *Call Bulletin* at the turn of the twentieth century, she married another reporter, Charles Norris. She had interviewed a number of famous people, including woman's rights activist Susan B. Anthony. Among her books were *Second Hand Wife* (1932) and *Beauty's Daughter* (1935). Her husband, Charles, had written a number of works on social problems, including *Seed* (1930), a novel about birth control. Charles's brother was Frank Norris, well-known author of the railroad exposé, *The Octopus* (1901). Kathleen Norris advocated temperance, and she and her husband had a country home in the Saratoga hills above Congress Springs as well as a home in Palo Alto.

Another popular literary figure was Ruth Comfort Mitchell, poet and author of over thirty books. She was a guest and presenter at To Kalon on a number of occasions during the 1930s and 40s. Los Gatos, her summer home, was the setting for some of her stories. She was Christian Scientist, and taught Sunday school for that church. She married Sanborn Young, a Republican California State Senator and founding vice-president of La Rinconada Country Club in 1929. The Youngs were close personal friends of the Herbert Hoovers, and entertained them in their Los Gatos home on a number of occasions, including while Hoover was President of the United States. Mitchell was a

To Kalon group boarding
a bus for a trip to the
Steinbeck House, 1993.

Carolyn McCoid (left)
and author James
Houston, with his book
Snow Mountain Passage,
Guest Day Tea, 2001.

contemporary of John Steinbeck, and she wrote a critical review of his *Grapes of Wrath*. But Steinbeck's books have also held the interest of To Kalon members; the club made excursions to Steinbeck House and library in Salinas in 1977, 1993, and 1999. The club was one of the first groups to visit the new Steinbeck Center.

Jeanne Wakatsuki and her husband, James Houston, co-authored *Farewell to Manzanar*, the true story of Jeanne's Japanese American family's internment during World War II. The book was published in 1973, and the couple gave a presentation to To Kalon in early 1975 at La Hacienda Restaurant in Los Gatos. Today the book has become a classic in California history and is required reading in many high schools. James Houston appeared again before To Kalon in 2001, to discuss his new historical novel about the infamous Donner Expedition, *Snow Mountain Passage*. He autographed copies of the book that had just hit bookstore shelves that very week.

Jewell Malm Newburn won an award in 1987 for *Pomo Dawn of Song*, poems about the Pomo Indians. She came before the club in a meeting at the Farrington House, just after the Loma Prieta Earthquake in 1989, and wrote a poem for the occasion:

**The Kirk-Farrington House**

*Theophilius Kirk, in 1878*
*Built a home in the style Italianate:*
*A farmhouse he shared with Lizzie, his wife,*
*One thousand acres of productive life.*

*Eight years later in '86,*
*Nature concocted a terrible fix:*
*When the year-long stream in front flowed by,*
*Five <u>miles</u> away jumped its course and went dry.*

*In 1989, we wait*
*For those who care to enter the gate*
*And hold the noble, Italianate farm*
*Safe from earthquake, fire and harm.*

*Sacred, silent…in its keep,*
*While the eye of the creek is closed in sleep.*

*—Jewell Malm Newburn*

## Fashion and Design

Some club members have had a talent for interior design. In the spring of 1912, Lulu (Mrs. Benjamin) Ledyard gave a program on the "Artistic Home," where she made suggestions about wall coverings, furnishings, and art. Several members with a talent for flower arranging gave presentations to the club. Longtime member Betty (Mrs. Richard) Wells, who had her own interior design business, spoke on several occasions. In November 1966, Richard Gump, of the famous and exclusive San Francisco store, Gumps, presented "Good Taste Costs No More." Gump had authored a book of the same title as

*Sue Casey (left) and Carol Boyce, in period costume.*

A fashion show of Pacific Rim costumes, collected by Zura Lindsay on her world travels. (Left to right) Ruth Hait, Ruth Hickey, Beth Lindsay, Frances Chapman, Zura Lindsay, Helen Issacson, and Alberta Boomer.

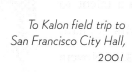

To Kalon field trip to San Francisco City Hall, 2001

the program, and offered the book for sale, which was "snatched up by the members."

Among dozens of fashions shows, the unusual ones live on in the memory of the members. Dorothy (Mrs. Theo) Farrington and Nita (Mrs. William) Binder cleverly presented the "Mad Hatters," showing off Farrington's amazing collection of four hundred hats. In the fall of 1961, Nita (Mrs. William) Binder hosted a fashion show entitled "A Tour of the Pacific" at Zura (Mrs. Curtis) Lindsay's home, featuring "many lovely oriental costumes collected" on her travels.[73] Some club members agreed to model grass skirts, floral leis, kimonos, and elaborate headdresses, while Mrs. Binder provided the

commentary. That particular program is still recalled as one of the all-time great afternoons for the club.

Programs have been the mainstay of the To Kalon Club. But as crucial as programs have been, they would not have been planned and executed without an inquiring membership. The membership desires good programs, appreciates them, and is willing to expend time, effort, and cash to coordinate them. According to Sue (Mrs. Richard) Casey, "I feel this organization has survived because the members are willing to take responsibility for being an officer or committee head without any complaint and they do a good job."[74] A diligent program chairwoman and committee is the key to strong programming which will ensure the future of the club.

*(Left to right) La Verne Randall, Sue Casey, Sue Bruntz, and Carol Shields, Spring Guest Day, 2000, at the San José Country Club.*

*Kay Walter (left) and Ruth Walsh at The Tech Museum of Innovation in San José, 1999.*

*(Left to right) Sue Casey, Charlene Snell, Sandy Stepovich, and Carol Boyce, Annual Picnic at Blair Ranch, 1993.*

*The Porter Building on Santa Clara and Second streets, San José.*
*The first meeting place for the Young Woman's Club was in the Porter Building.*
Courtesy of History San José.

# CHAPTER SIX

## Meeting Places

OVER THE PAST ONE HUNDRED YEARS, the To Kalon Club has met in a variety of venues, ranging from individual homes and churches to historical landmarks and public parks. Since the mid-1930s when the club's modest building fund was decimated by a bank failure, the club has made no effort to procure a clubhouse. The location of meetings, programs, and annual events has taken on significance in itself; the choices mirror local political, social, and environmental history. The development and re-development of downtown San José, the rise and demise of city parks, and the ebb and flow of a changing economy are reflected in the locations of the To Kalon gatherings.

The first meeting place of the Young Woman's Club was the Porter Building on Santa Clara Street at the northeast corner of Second. It was the largest building in San José at the time, and the newspaper claimed that "during an average business day as many as 3,500 people visit the various offices" there.[75] It was particularly popular for doctors, dentists, and attorneys, a few of whom had daughters on the membership list of the Young Woman's Club. The building boasted a new "Otis rapid elevator taking the passengers to any floor in a few seconds." The Young Woman's Club paid $1 per month rent for meeting space there, plus the cost of coal for heating.

The club also took advantage of the nearby Unitarian Church at 160 North Third

> "...the ebb and flow of a changing economy are reflected in the locations of the To Kalon gatherings."

Street. Designed in 1892 by Architect George W. Page who had designed several other important San José buildings, including the Hayes Mansion and some large homes on The Alameda, the church was constructed in the Romanesque Revival style. The circular sanctuary symbolizes its egalitarian philosophy. The Unitarian Church was an important venue for many women's gatherings in San José, partly because its precepts included equal rights for women. Both the San José Woman's Club and the Young Woman's Club were welcomed at the Unitarian Church.

The church was the site of the very first program for the Young Woman's Club. At its "initial reception" in 1903 as the newspaper noted, one hundred young ladies were welcomed and entertained at the Unitarian Church parlors. Both the large and small parlors were "transformed by their wealth of flowers and foliage," and "streamers of scarlet ribbon were caught with bunches of red berries." Soloists entertained, including a male vocalist, Mr. Hadley Lawrence. The newspaper reported that "it may be safely predicted that the Young Woman's Club will be a factor in San José society" in the coming years.[76] The club paid $6 for the use of the church parlors for their first event.[77]

The Unitarian Church was also the headquarters for a convention of the California Federation of Woman's Clubs, which met in San José in 1906. Several local women's clubs, including the YWC, hosted the large gathering of two hundred delegates from around the state. Local businesses loaned twelve automobiles to ferry the women from the train station to the Vendome and the St. James hotels.[78] Carrie Stevens Walter, the owner and editor of the monthly newspaper *Santa Clara*,[79] wrote an extensive article for the San José *Mercury and Herald*.[80] Walter was a member of the San José Woman's Club and the mother of YWC member Mary Walter.

Her article identified five main topics on the agenda for discussion at the convention. They included "Advantages of Federation," "Programs for Small Clubs," "Study Clubs," "How Can This Year Be Made More Helpful?" and "Would a Biennial Election Prove Advantageous to our State?"[81] One of the reasons that the federation was successful was that it did not advocate a single issue, such as suffrage, but discussed a wide array of topics of interest to early twentieth century women.

Each afternoon of the convention, from 4:30 until 5:30, tea was served at the San José Woman's Clubhouse on Third Street. YWC and woman's club members took turns hostessing. During other breaks from the business of the day, excursions were available for the delegates from around the state, including touring the local court house and Hall of Records, an auto trip to Agnew where the State Asylum for the Chronic Insane was located, and the oyster beds and marina of Alviso. Mrs. Hugh Center, an active member of the woman's club, was on the excursions committee. On another day, delegates toured Mission Santa Clara and Santa Clara College where they were greeted by the president of the school, the Reverend Robert Kenna, S.J., and visited the College of the Pacific and the State Normal School. At the end of the week, they took excursions to Congress Springs in Saratoga and Alum Rock Park, too.

The crowning glory of the convention was a grand ball held at the Vendome Hotel attended by about 1,500 guests. Edith (Miss) MacChesney, president of the Young Woman's Club, wore "a dainty gray voile, worn over silk, and having touches of gold and white,"[82] as she greeted guests in the receiving line. The reception committee also included "the Misses Helen Stocking, and Florence Granger."[83]

The convention was deemed a grand success, and club members took great

*The Vendome Hotel on North First Street in San José was the most luxurious hotel in the city. It was razed in 1930.*

Photograph from *The Road of A Thousand Wonders*, a 1908 publication of the Southern Pacific Company.

satisfaction in showing off their city and the Santa Clara Valley. The Vendome Hotel provided a perfect social venue, while the Unitarian Church allowed the real business to be accomplished. Today the Unitarian Church is often used as a community center, has recovered from a devastating fire in 1995, and is listed as a California Historical Landmark.

The San José Woman's Club procured a clubhouse at 43 South Third Street in 1906. It had been the Leddy family home. The woman's club made some changes to it to accommodate club functions, and allowed the YWC the use of a second floor room. Ledgers reflect rent paid for the use of the clubhouse. The young women had participated in and supported fundraisers for their mothers' clubhouse, and were happy to reap the benefits of those efforts.

The same year that the house was purchased, the YWC held a Halloween party there. Laura (Miss) Bailey was the hostess, and the refreshments were pumpkin pie, cider, sandwiches, apples and marshmallows. All were "served at prettily set tables in <u>our own club room</u>…. The day was warm enough to wear my organdie dress."[84] Bailey also noted that, "the fortune teller, a professional, was really uncanny in her powers." The emphasis placed on <u>our own club room</u>, underlined in the minutes book, indicates how pleased club members were to have a reliable and consistent meeting place.

There were some problems with the meeting space, however. In 1907, the YWC was forced to use another room because a recital had been planned in the room ordinarily rented to it. The room was cold, and the recital could be heard throughout the presentation on Milton. The young women tried to bear with the inconvenience and "seemed to enjoy" the meeting "in spite of the untoward circumstances."[85]

By about 1913, the minutes from YWC meetings indicate the beginnings of a separation from the San José Woman's Club. The younger women used the older club's house less often, and the ledger for 1915 indicates rent paid to the woman's club, along with a fine. Beginning in 1916, the YWC met at the new Young Women's Christian Association (YWCA) building that was completed that year at Second and San Antonio streets. The four-story building was designed by renowned architect Julia Morgan, designer of Hearst Castle among several other California landmarks. Besides providing housing for San José State College women, it also provided meeting space for women's clubs, including the Young Woman's Club. Most meetings in 1916-17 were held at the new building, for which they paid $2.50 per month room rental.

Social changes during the 1920s are reflected in the tenor of To Kalon Club meetings. The gatherings became decidedly more social, and the programs were seldom presented by club members. In January 1920, the *Mercury and Herald* reported that the most recent meeting of To Kalon was "one of the most delightful in the history of the club and instead of the pleasant educational and more or less serious afternoons, the members assembled at the ever attractive Country Club and there enjoyed luncheon and a few hours of bridge." The following four meetings were scheduled for the Normal School (San José State), as a series of lectures by a Stanford professor on Modern English Drama.[86]

But determining an acceptable meeting place became more and more challenging.

The club began meeting in individual homes, and at the same time established its own fund to procure a clubhouse. The San José Woman's Club had a new building erected on south Eleventh Street, but To Kalon met there only occasionally. On October 10, 1929, To Kalon presented a painting by California artist Calthea Vivian to the woman's club. At that same meeting, Mrs. Hugh Brown gave a reading of "Jenny Lind."

During the last forty years of the twentieth century, the Calvary Methodist Church in the Rose Garden neighborhood of San José became the venue of choice for To Kalon meetings. The church's adjacent meeting room, Dr. James Strayer Hall, provides a convenient setting in a familiar neighborhood with plenty of parking. The church hall is not the only location for meetings, however. In 1995-1996, meetings were held in

*Calvary Methodist Church, 2002.*
Photographs by the author.

*Dr. James Strayer Hall, Calvary Methodist Church, 2002.*

different historical buildings around the valley, including the Hayes Mansion, the Headen-Inman House and the Jamison-Brown House, Town Club, Kirk-Farrington House, the San José Historical Museum, Ainsley House, Wood-haven House, and the San José Country Club. Some To Kalon members have special relationships to these buildings, having been instrumental in donating them to the community.

## Annual Picnic

Every spring the To Kalon Club holds an annual picnic to culminate the club year, and as Helen (Mrs. Robert) Moore explained, it was a very important event. It "was sitting down and eating properly," not a casual affair. Members often brought their own china and silver service, along with freshly pressed table linens. The traditional "dressing up" was the expected attire for the day.

*Marjolie Thomas (left), Marsha Hall (center) and Colleen Lund, Spring Guest Day, 2001, San José Country Club.*

The annual picnic was held at a number of different sites over the years, but among the earliest was Alum Rock Park. The park had been part of a land grant to El Pueblo de San José in 1778, just one year after the pueblo itself was established. The park was surveyed in 1866, and four hundred acres was set aside as a park by California's legislature in 1872. At one time it was as large as 1,000 acres, but today contains just over seven hundred. San José's first and largest park, is the oldest city park in California.

Alum Rock Park earned its name for a 200-foot rock exuding a mineral compound called alum. Penitencia Creek runs through it. The one-time home to Ohlone Indians is ringed by rugged ridges offering spectacular views of the entire Santa Clara Valley. The park gives visitors the feeling of being far out in the wilderness because the deep canyon running through the two high ridges allows for distinct and isolated natural plant and wildlife habitats. The southern exposure has California black oak, madrone, and California buckeye, and is occupied by bobcats. The other canyon holds live oak and sustains black-tailed deer, rabbits, quail, red tailed hawks, and vultures.

A highway from San José to the Alum Rock Park was constructed in 1866 and a narrow gauge traction railway ran along it. The rail line was electrified and later transformed into a broad-gauge system.[87] Trains ran between downtown and the park every half hour, making it an extremely popular outing. The Alum Rock Railway was operated by Scotland native Hugh Center. He also purchased the San José and Santa Clara Railway, and converted the entire network from steam to electricity. The second railway ran down Santa Clara Street to The Alameda and on to Santa Clara. His railways were one of the first electric railways West of the Mississippi. Hugh Center's son, Hugh Stuart Center, eventually practiced law in San José.

*A woman boards the Alum Rock Steam Railroad in Alum Rock Park, circa 1900.*
Courtesy of History San José.

Alum Rock Park was one of San José's most treasured leisure spots and tourist destinations. The mineral springs drew visitors from all over the world, seeking out their restorative powers. There were both men's and women's sulfur springs bath houses. Over time, the hotel was complemented by a restaurant, dance pavilion, Japanese tea garden, and children's play areas. In 1914, a huge "natatorium," or covered swimming pool, was built with an enormous tile slide and high diving platforms. The pool addition cost upwards of $78,000.[88]

The park was a popular spot for the YWC to hold its annual picnics from 1903 until 1929. In May 1907, for example, the young women took the 10 a.m. streetcar out of San José to the park and enjoyed an "elaborate banquet" after their business meeting. A hike in the park to Alum Rock Falls was, as local writer Patricia Loomis noted, "a dress-up affair."[89]

Congress Springs, just above Saratoga, also had mineral springs and the water was bottled and sold throughout California. It was named after Congress Springs outside Saratoga, New York, because the mineral composition of the water was the same as its eastern counterpart. A popular hotel was built there, and late in the nineteenth century, was considered a health spa. Locals flocked to picnic on the seven-hundred-acre resort, and the Peninsular Railroad connected directly to it. A network of railroad track spread out from San José to all the Santa Clara County towns, and by the 1920s was about one hundred miles of track.[90] In 1903, the hotel burned and was not rebuilt, but the grounds, springs, and picnic areas remained popular destinations until the railroad stopped running there in 1932.

To Kalon Club members have often hosted annual picnics at family ranches scattered around Santa Clara Valley. One of the first excursions for the YWC was an all day

*Entrance to Alum Rock Park by road and by rail, circa 1900.*
Photograph by Jno. O. Tucker, courtesy of the Sourisseau Academy, San Jose State University.

affair at the Evans Ranch, on the old Tularcitos Rancho, near Milpitas. The property had been developed by Josiah Evans, grandfather of club member Nellie Evans. Nellie's sister, Elizabeth, recalled the event in a letter written years later:

> a stream ran through the backyard and close to this creek were planted fig trees…They were the black mission fig and spread their roots throughout the backyard like a banyan tree. As many of the members had no way of getting to our place, one of the hay wagons known as a clipper bed was closely padded with hay and boxes, and the members were met at the Southern Pacific Station in Milpitas by the hired man driver and thusly transported the two mile ride to our home. I can hear to this day the laughing crowd that climbed down from the hay wagon.[91]

Member Celia (Mrs. Everett) Bailey mentioned, "Y.W. Club party at Nellie Evans. Train to Milpitas then fruit wagon to ranch. Sky parlor under big fig tree…Delicious refreshments—cream berries, etc."[92] Then she went on, "they gathered beneath the old fig trees where there were many small tables and colored table cloths. Creamed chicken was served over hot biscuits etc strawberries and cream coffee etc.… After the picnic the members lolled about in hammocks hung from the limbs of the trees. Chinese lanterns gayly [sic] hung about."

In October 1908 the YWC met at the A. E. Wilder ranch in the hills above Los Gatos. Cynthia (Tibbetts) Wilder's husband was the cashier of the Bank of Los Gatos. Sixteen club members arrived in the morning, and spent a few hours playing "tennis, sewing, reading, and talking. At 1 o'clock an elaborate picnic lunch was spread in a grove near the house and most of the afternoon was spent under the oaks."[93] Two letters from club moderator Louise (Mrs. Stephen) Jones, who was away in Illinois, were read. The young women were so impressed with the letters that they took a vote deciding that each would write a note in response.

On a number of occasions, the club met at the Arthur Curtner ranch near Warm Springs. It was part of a vast 8,000 acres belonging at one time to Arthur's father, Henry. Arthur was the vice-president of Osen Motors, a Dodge dealership on North First Street. In May 1918, the club women "motored out to the country home of Mrs. Arthur Curtner."[94] In May 1932, the annual picnic was held there again. Edna B.(Mrs. Arthur) Curtner was also active in Eastfield, and had served as its president.

The Coe Ranch was a popular venue for To Kalon annual picnics during the 1960s and 70s. Pat Coe was a To Kalon member, and her husband, Henry S. Coe, owned the working horse and cattle ranch. At one time their ranch was part of Rancho San Felipe, known to early Californians as *Los Huecos* (rolling hills and valleys). The mission-style home on the property was built by Henry's parents in 1928.[95] The ranch also featured some original outbuildings, an 1865-vintage ranch house, a smithy, and a barn. Pat Coe's daughter, Winifred Coe Verbica, recalled To Kalon meetings there and that her "mom delighted entertaining the group—the larger the better!" Club member Nancy Drew noted that Pat "was always so gracious and thoughtful. She would greet <u>each</u> person at every meeting. It was always a great occasion to go out to the ranch."[96]

Marian (Mrs. Martell) Blair's ranch was the venue for many To Kalon annual picnics. The sprawling ranch near the Calero Dam in the south part of the county was

*Marian Blair (left) and Lois Brown, hostesses at the annual picnic at Blair Ranch, 1989.*

Liz Smrekar, Bev Mangan (center), and Marty Lion, Annual Picnic at the Blair Ranch, 1999.

a rustic setting where a large lake was visible from the yard. Some husbands of club members acted as parking attendants, so the ladies could valet their cars upon arrival at the Blairs. In the recent survey of club members, Marian's hospitality for the annual picnic is mentioned dozens of time.

San José's hotels have been the setting for memorable events in To Kalon history. The city's original elegant hotel, the Vendome Hotel, opened in 1889 on eleven acres of the former Josiah Belden estate on North First Street. "The large, airy, wooden structure, surrounded by a scene of natural and created beauty,"[97] had 150 guest rooms in four stories. The hotel cost $300,000 to construct and featured a "plunge," a billiard room, barber shop, ballroom, several dining rooms, ladies' parlors, and an elevator. Outside there was a nine-hole golf course, tennis courts, and livery stables. A two story annex was added in 1903, but it collapsed in the 1906 earthquake.

Among many YWC events held at the Vendome were the 1908 New Year's Party and a 1921 charity ball. Socialite Mary Bowden Carroll, in her 1903 book *Ten Years in Paradise*, described the Vendome this way:

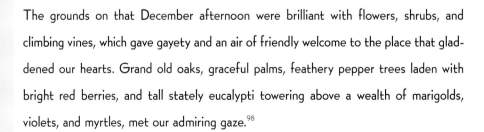

The grounds on that December afternoon were brilliant with flowers, shrubs, and climbing vines, which gave gayety and an air of friendly welcome to the place that gladdened our hearts. Grand old oaks, graceful palms, feathery pepper trees laden with bright red berries, and tall stately eucalypti towering above a wealth of marigolds, violets, and myrtles, met our admiring gaze.[98]

The elegant old hotel was sold in 1930,[99] razed and subdivided. But during its forty year history, it was the queen of Victorian propriety. The newspaper announced the hotel's death knell in this way:

> Like an old lady in a time dimmed shawl of gray, her pointed tortoise shell combs silhouetted against the draperies of the sky, the Vendome sits today among her skirts of oak and lawn and bright flower beds—sits and broods, perhaps over the 'gay nineties,' watching with dim, old eyes the ghost parade of the thousands who have enjoyed her hospitality.[100]

After 1926, the Hotel Sainte Claire usurped the Vendome as the first choice of San José's high society. The elegant hotel built by developer T. S. Montgomery, cost over $1 million, an astronomical sum for the time. No expense was spared in the terra cotta, coral and henna-colored decorations and antique walnut furnishings, many imported from Europe. Will Rogers, at one time a hotel guest, was said to have quipped, "Looks like this here hotel outgrew the town."[101] The hotel represented the town's aspirations to reach new heights of social and economic success in California.

*Dining room of the Hotel Sainte Claire, circa 1950. The hotel was the venue of dozens of To Kalon Club events over the years.*

Courtesy of History San José.

The To Kalon Club used the hotel for many events, but the most memorable was a January 7, 1932, a musical tea. Three hundred eighty members, guests and escorts arrived at the Hotel Sainte Claire's elegant ballroom to hear baritone Douglas Beattie accompanied by To Kalon's own Wilna (Mrs. Floyd) Parton. The following year, in 1932, about 160 members and guests gathered in the lounge of the Hotel Sainte Claire for a slightly more modest event. The Hotel Sainte Claire suffered the same drop in popularity that the Vendome had, but the building was not torn down. During the 1970s, the building was a low-rent boarding house with a very high crime rate. It was purchased and redeveloped into a modern version of its original self in the 1990s, and today is one of downtown's important hotels operated by the Hyatt Corporation.

The De Anza Hotel, built in 1931 by the Carl Swenson Company, was also a popular venue for visitors to the city and local society events. Throughout the 1930s, its upper crust clientele transformed into servicemen and local girls during the war years. Many romances were begun in the Danzabar Room at the De Anza. Among the celebrities who checked into the hotel were Fred MacMurray, Susan Hayward, First Lady Eleanor Roosevelt, and young actor Mickey Rooney. To Kalon held several lunches at the hotel. Today it is owned by the family of To Kalon member Martha (Mrs. Jerome) Kozlowski.

LoCurto's Gardens, near a neighborhood popularly known as "Goosetown" on Almaden Road, was a night club sitting on nine-and-a-half acres where big name performers dazzled San José from the 1920s until the 1950s. Variously called LoCurto's, Olympian Gardens, Hawaiian Gardens, and finally Italian Gardens, it was raided in 1935, and the authorities accused the proprietors of running a casino there. Sixty surprised San Joséans were locked down under house arrest while the police scoured the premises. Nevertheless, it remained a very popular spot for nightlife, and To Kalon held events there. As one club member quipped, it was "the nearest thing to a night club that San José could boast of for many years."[102]

Club members have offered their homes for club programs as well. For many years, when members were primarily young mothers, there was a "baby party" each year, where members brought their children and organized games and activities for them. In 1910 and in 1914 it was at (Mrs. Oliver) Blanchard's on University Avenue. In 1922, it was at the home of Edna B. (Mrs. Arthur) Curtner at Warm Springs. About forty children attended and some performed vocal and musical pieces.

From the earliest years, the YWC and later To Kalon held an annual "Colonial Tea" to celebrate George Washington's birthday. The members donned elaborate costumes and powdered their hair to portray the founding fathers. In 1917 the Colonial Tea was held at The Alameda home of Mrs. Cora Hatch Johnston. The *Mercury Herald* reported that "Japanese plum blossoms in artistic profusion lent the charm of their

*Programs from "Children's Day" at the home of Mrs. Arthur Curtner, 1922. Each program cover was hand-drawn.*

*Colonial Tea of the Young Woman's Club held at the San Jose Woman's Clubhouse in 1907.*

La Verne Schmidt (left), Masel Sheehan (center) and Ginny Brownton, at Allied Arts in Menlo Park, 1999.

Fuji Takaichi, at the Villages, 1978.

fragrance to the animated scene, while the glow of daintily-shaded candles gave an added charm to the powdered hair and handsome colonial costumes worn by the ladies present."[103]

Activities other than the annual picnic called for slightly different accommodations. Card parties or luncheons were held at the San José Country Club (1932), the Los Altos County Club (1936), the Almaden Country Club (1956), the Hyatt House (1969) and The Villages on several occasions. The Allied Arts Guild in Menlo Park has been a popular venue for To Kalon gatherings since the 1940s, including its annual picnic in 1946. The buildings were constructed in 1929 as a consortium supporting local artists. Since 1951 it has been owned by the Woodside-Atherton Auxiliary, a fundraising group for the Lucile Salter Packard Children's Hospital. It was closed in 2002 for extensive renovations to the mission-style, tile-roofed buildings.

The venues of To Kalon events and gatherings give a setting to both club history and county history. Choices about where to hold a club event show what locations, in a given period of time, were the most popular or convenient. It is unlikely that a contemporary meeting or picnic of the club would be held at Alum Rock Park or the Italian Gardens. But the Hotel Sainte Claire and the De Anza Hotel have both experienced a resurgence of their one-time prominence downtown. Although the Allied Arts Guild is currently closed, the club is likely to schedule events there when it is reopened. To Kalon Club history is bolstered with color and depth when placed in the setting of these many venues.

# CONCLUSION

# Adjournment

AS WE ADJOURN TO EMBARK UPON THE NEXT ONE HUNDRED YEARS, we contemplate a few questions posed by this history. How has the To Kalon Club survived one hundred years? It has not only survived, but thrived because it is steeped in local history, rooted in networks of family relationships, and revolves around a desire for intellectual stimulation.

Another obvious question that demands asking is: can the club live on for another century? Younger women are not often available to join, but sometimes come to guest days. After all, a woman in her forties today may be venturing into motherhood for the first time. One hundred years ago, she may well have been approaching grand motherhood at the same age.

Evidently, youth is not the only reason for a club's viability. Current membership sits at its capacity of sixty. The club has incurred no debt, supports no overhead, and owes no mortgage. Even clubs that own a clubhouse are compelled to maintain it, which can be a costly endeavor. To Kalon has no such burden. It has not focused on acquisition or ownership, but on inquiry and knowledge. Its membership is older because in today's world, professional women do not have time beyond their careers and families until they are older.

"Continued success in enhancing the lives of others through knowledge and friendship."

*Linda Fish (left), Carol Boyce (center), and Sue Bruntz, Annual Meeting, 2002, Rinconada Hills Clubhouse.*

Lois McDonald (left), Huette James (center), and Nancy Drew, Christmas guest Day Tea, 1995.

Among the most consistent comments about To Kalon from current members is that the meetings and programs have been a respite from the demands of modern life. As member Huette James recalled, the club meetings were "civilized and the members so gracious." She said, "it took us out of the hustle bustle, we could relax and be ourselves. And we'd learn something!"[104]

Members also greatly appreciated bringing information from club meetings home to share at their dinner tables. Several members, whose mothers were members before them, mentioned hearing about very interesting programs and of cultural or literary ideas at the dinner table. The family benefited from a mother's participation in the club.

The To Kalon Club is very different from the Young Woman's Club established in 1903. Those charter members would not recognize today's club as their own. By the time the club was fifty years old, its structure had been formalized, and over time, the membership has redefined its purpose and goals. The most obvious change was that almost no members were making presentations to the club; programs were offered by paid artists or speakers, with a decided focus on cultural arts. The membership included a wider range of women from more diverse backgrounds. In 1996-97, members were asked to wear nametags at meetings, a sure sign that membership had expanded beyond the original enclave of important families.

Members value their experiences in the To Kalon Club. Caren (Mrs. Christopher) Hebeler, a fourth generation member, gave good wishes to the club as it approached its one hundredth birthday: "Continued success in enhancing the lives of others through knowledge and friendship." Another member, Sandy (Mrs. Alex) Stepovich, articulated the feelings of many when she stated:

> To Kalon—without a doubt—is my most "favorite" of any organization I have been a part of. It has provided leadership opportunities and programs that have introduced so many new subjects that I would normally not know about. It has brought about years of conversations with family and friends about the programs and ideas learned. To Kalon's membership has always been of outstanding women. It is a pleasure to be surrounded by these women from many walks of life.[105]

*Carmine Davy (left) and Ruby Nikirk at the Hyatt House in 1972. Mrs. Nikirk was a charter member of the Young Woman's Club in 1903.*

As long as women gather to inquire, to explore, and to develop their fullest capacities, then there will be another "meeting of the minds," and the club will survive.

**Susan Andersen**
(Mrs. William)
*Joined 1997-98*

**Betty Bocks**
(Mrs. Charles)
*Joined 1992-93*

**Carol Boyce**
(Mrs. Thomas)
*Joined 1986-97*

**Virginia Brownton**
(Mrs. William)
*Joined 1964-65*

**Susan Bruntz**
(Mrs. G. Clayton)
*Joined 1991-92*

**Sue Casey**
(Mrs. Richard)
*Joined 1987-88*

**Nancy Drew**
(Mrs. John)
*Joined 1987-88*

**Beverly Fehler**
(Mrs. Donald)
*Joined 1979-80*

**Linda Fish**
(Mrs. Richard)
*Joined 2001-02*

**Lonna Franklin**
(Mrs. Donald)
*Joined 1996-1997*

**Susan Grundman**
(Mrs. Ronald)
*Joined 2000-01*

**Ruth Guderian**
(Mrs. A. M.)
*Joined 1997-98*

**Marcia Hall**
(Mrs. Marshall)
*Joined 1976-77*

**Edna Harrison**
(Mrs. Richard)
*Joined 1997-98*

**JoAnn Herring**
(Mrs. Jack)
*Joined 1986-87*

**JoAnne Hersch**
(Mrs. Robert)
*Joined 1999-00*

**Gerry Hicks**
(Mrs. Robert)
*Joined 1982-83*

**Huette James**
(Mrs. Robert)
*Joined 1969-70*

**Betty Kirtland**
(Mrs. John A.)
*Joined 1980-81*

**Martha Kozlowski**
(Mrs. Jerome)
*Joined 1997-98*

**Henne Kropf**
(Mrs. Karl)
*Joined 1987-88*

**Marion Langley**
(Mrs. Marion Atkinson)
*Joined 1960-61; 1982-83*

**Marty Lion**
(Mrs. Paul)
*Joined 1990-91*

**Jane Lucid**
(Mrs. Morgan)
*Joined 2000-01*

A Meeting of the Minds

**Carol Luckhardt**
(Mrs. John)
*Joined 1974-75*

**Colleen M. Lund**
(Mrs. Colleen M.)
*Joined 1989-90*

**Beverly Mangan**
(Mrs. Leo)
*Joined 1994-95*

**Millie McBrian**
(Mrs. Jim)
*Joined 2000-01*

**Ann McCoid**
(Mrs. Stephen)
*Joined 2002*

**Carolyn McCoid**
(Mrs. Dean)
*Joined 1996-97*

**Lois McDonald**
(Mrs. Richard)
*Joined 1971-72*

**Margaret McNelly**
(Mrs. Malcolm)
*Joined 1997-98*

**Mimi Oneal**
(Mrs. Dan)
*Joined 1989-90*

**Shirley Oneal**
(Mrs. Louis)
*Joined 1968-69*

**Nancy O'Neill**
(Mrs. Richard)
*Joined 1989-90*

**Alice Orth**
(Mrs. James)
*Joined 1985-86*

**Nancy Parton**
(Mrs. William A.)
*Joined 1975-76*

**Joanne Petersen**
(Mrs. Fred)
*Joined 1977-78*

**Jesse Peterson**
(Mrs. Robert)
*Joined 1995-96*

**LaVerne Randall**
(Mrs. Robert)
*Joined 1993-94*

**Jo Ann Risko**
(Mrs. William)
*Joined 2001-02*

**Betty Roberts**
(Mrs. E. W.)
*Joined 1988-89*

**Beryl Rodenbaugh**
(Mrs. Hase)
*Joined 1997-98*

**La Verne Schmidt**
(Mrs. Gerald)
*Joined 1987-88*

**Joan Scott**
(Mrs. Gerald)
*Joined 1979-80*

**Masel Sheehan**
(Mrs. Richard)
*Joined 1996-97*

**Carol Shields**
(Mrs. Richard)
*Joined 1997-98*

**Karen Shirey**
(Mrs. Fred)
*Joined 1999-00*

**Nancy Short**
(Mrs. Charles A.)
*Joined 1980-81*

**Phyllis Simpkins**
(Mrs. Alan)
*Joined 1994-95*

**Joanne Skillicorn**
(Mrs. Stanley)
*Joined 1985-86*

**Ditty Smith**
(Mrs. Leonard)
*Joined 1994-95*

**Liz Smrekar**
(Mrs. Jack)
*Joined 1996-97*

**Charlene Snell**
(Mrs. George)
*Joined 1987-88*

**Sandy Stepovich**
(Mrs. Alex)
*Joined 1978-79*

**Marjolie Thomas**
(Mrs. Mark)
*Joined 1987-88*

Kay Walter
(Mrs. Allan M.)
*Joined 1970-71*

Ann Williamson
(Mrs. Robert)
*Joined 2001-02*

Ann Wright
(Mrs. H. M.)
*Joined 2002*

## Associate Members

June (Mrs. Donald E.) Bischoff

Marian (Mrs H. Martell) Blair

Lois (Mrs. George) Brown

Dianne (Mrs. Stanley) Chinchen

Mary (Mrs. Barton)Collins

Doris (Mrs. William) Drennan

Ellie (Mrs. Donald) Fischer

Shirley (Mrs. Jack) Fischer

Bobbe (Mrs. Glenn) George

Caren (Mrs. Christopher) Hebeler

Patty (Mrs. Henry L.) Imsen

Elizabeth (Mrs. Eugene) Jung

Soo (Mrs. Bruce) Krogstad

Ruth Ann (Mrs. Robert) McFarlane

Julie (Mrs. Douglas) Moore

Jean (Mrs. David) Schrader

Helen (Mrs. Charles) Timpany

Ruth (Mrs. Stephen) Walsh

Betty (Mrs. Richard G.) Wells

Mary Frances (Mrs. Burton K.) Wines

# Club Presidents

## Young Woman's Club

| | |
|---|---|
| 1903 | Genevieve (Miss) Chambers |
| 1904 | Genevieve (Miss) Chambers, Edith (Miss) MacChesney |
| 1905 | Edith (Miss) MacChesney |
| 1906 | Ruby (Miss) Brooks |
| 1907 | Nellie (Miss) Evans |
| 1908 | Ellen (Miss) Potter |
| 1909 | Ella (Miss) Brady |
| 1910 | Martha (Miss) Chase |
| 1911 | Maude (Mrs.) Miller Graves |
| 1912 | Dorothy (Miss) Donovan |
| 1913 | Nellie (Miss) Evans |
| 1914 | Manette (Mrs. Orren) Harlan |
| 1915 | (Mrs. Lou) Smith |
| 1916 | (Mrs. Charles) Parkinson |
| 1917 | (Mrs. Arthur) Langford |

## To Kalon Club

| | |
|---|---|
| 1918 | Maude (Mrs. Fred) Curtiss |
| 1919 | Clara (Mrs. Leonard) Edwards |
| 1920 | (Mrs. Willard) Hayden |
| 1921 | Cora (Mrs.) Hatch Johnston |
| 1922 | (Mrs. Avenal) Ross |
| 1923 | (Mrs. Newell) Bullock |
| 1924 | Rae (Mrs. Earnest) Pieper |
| 1925 | (Mrs. Herbert) Jones |
| 1926 | Grace (Mrs. Harvey) Herold |
| 1927 | Cora (Mrs. Albert) Foster |
| 1928 | Genevieve (Mrs. Frank) Campbell |
| 1929 | (Mrs. Harold) Chase |
| 1930 | Azalea (Mrs. Earl) Alderman |
| 1931 | Bernice (Mrs. Henri) Hill |
| 1932 | (Mrs. John) Hunt Shephard |
| 1933 | Ruth (Mrs. Arthur) Butcher |
| 1934 | Trix (Mrs. Walter) Wilcox |

| | |
|---|---|
| 1935 | Alice (Mrs. Charles) Richards |
| 1936 | Alta (Mrs. Cecil) Burchfield |
| 1937 | DeEtte (Mrs. E. N.) Richmond |
| 1938 | Zura (Mrs. Curtis) Lindsay |
| 1939 | (Mrs. Chester) Perry |
| 1940 | Helen (Mrs. Burnell) Richmond |
| 1941 | Wilma (Mrs. Floyd) Parton |
| 1942 | (Mrs. E. J.) Pellier |
| 1943 | Alice (Mrs. Charles) Luckhardt |
| 1944 | (Mrs. Charles) Braslan |
| 1945 | Effie (Mrs. Harold) Hunt |
| 1946 | Dorothy (Miss) Donovan |
| 1947 | Gladys (Mrs. Everett) Myers |
| 1948 | Vi (Mrs. Eugene) Lawrence |
| 1949 | Lillian (Mrs.) Roberts |
| 1950 | Patty (Mrs. Duncan) Oneal |
| 1951 | Lydia (Mrs. Walter) Crider |
| 1952 | Alice (Mrs. M. V.) McDonald |

| | | | |
|---|---|---|---|
| 1953 | Marian (Mrs. David) Atkinson | 1971 | Wilma (Mrs. Walter) Borchers |
| 1954 | Byrdie (Mrs. E. Ryan) Booker | 1972 | Frances (Mrs. Anthony) Hamann |
| 1955 | Genevieve (Mrs. Adrien) Lassere | 1973 | Carolyn (Mrs. James) Iglehart |
| 1956 | Helen (Mrs. Robert) Moore | 1974 | Marian (Mrs. H. Martell) Blair |
| 1957 | Marian (Mrs. Ralph) Shafor | 1975 | Emily (Mrs. Ernest) Renzel, Jr. |
| 1958 | Lois (Mrs. Arthur) Caldwell | 1976 | Mary Frances (Mrs. Burton) Wines |
| 1959 | Miriam (Mrs. Don) Parker | 1977 | Toddy (Mrs. Henry) Dahleen |
| 1960 | Ruth (Mrs. Frank) Hickey | 1978 | Mildred (Mrs. Charles) Kennedy |
| 1961 | Clara (Mrs. Leonard) Edwards | 1979 | Carol (Mrs. John) Luckhardt |
| 1962 | Leah (Mrs.) Watts | 1980 | Lois (Mrs.George) Brown |
| 1963 | Betty (Mrs. Richard) Wells | 1981 | Julie (Mrs. R. Douglas) Moore |
| 1964 | Nita (Mrs. William) Binder | 1982 | Mary (Mrs. Barton) Collins |
| 1965 | Beth (Mrs. Wesley) Lindsay | 1983 | Lois (Mrs. Richard) McDonald |
| 1966 | Hazel (Mrs. Mark) Hopkins, Jr. | 1984 | Joan (Mrs. Gerald) Scott |
| 1967 | Sarah (Mrs. John) Dowdle | 1985 | Shirley (Mrs. Louis) Oneal |
| 1968 | Ruth (Mrs. John) Bohnett | 1986 | Sandy (Mrs. Alex) Stepovich |
| 1969 | Elizabeth (Mrs. Eugene) Jung | 1987 | Betty (Mrs. John) Kirtland |
| 1970 | Ginny (Mrs. William) Brownton | 1988 | Doris (Mrs. William) Drennan |

| | |
|---|---|
| 1989 | Nancy (Mrs. William) Parton |
| 1990 | Nancy (Mrs. Charles) Short, Jr. |
| 1991 | Alice (Mrs. James) Orth |
| 1992 | Carol (Mrs. Thomas) Boyce |
| 1993 | Joann (Mrs. Jack) Herring |
| 1994 | LaVerne (Mrs. Gerald) Schmidt |
| 1995 | Huette (Mrs. Robert) James |
| 1996 | Nancy (Mrs. John) Drew |
| 1997 | Mimi (Mrs. Dan) Oneal |
| 1998 | Joanne (Mrs. Fred) Petersen |
| 1999 | Sue (Mrs. Clayton) Bruntz |
| 2000 | Colleen (Mrs.) Lund |
| 2001 | Marty (Mrs. Paul) Lion, Jr. |
| 2002 | Sue (Mrs. Richard) Casey |

# Endnotes

1 *Webster's Third International Dictionary*, 1965.

2 San Jose *Mercury*, 20 September 1903, 19/4.

3 Ibid., 11 October 1903, 18/2.

4 Anne Ruggles Gere, *Intimate Practices: Literacy and Cultural Work in U. S. Women's Clubs* (Chicago: University of Illinois Press, 1997), 5.

5 Theodora Penny Martin, *The Sound of our Own Voices: Women's Study Clubs 1860-1910* (Boston: Beacon Press, 1987), 3.

6 Mrs. E. E. H. McNeil, Mrs. A.B. Clement, Mrs. J. Schoenheit, Mrs. E. O. Smith, Mrs. A. A. Leffler, Miss R. English, Mrs. N. A. Sanders, Mrs. G.W. Northern, Miss F. M. Easterbrook.

7 *Mercury*, 29 December 1992.

8 Helen (Schoenheit) Moore, interview with the author, 19 June 2000. Los Gatos, California.

9 Bertha M. Rice, *The Women of our Valley, Vol. I* (San Jose, CA: Bertha Rice), 115.

10 Ibid., 31.

11 *Mercury*, 28 August 1903.

12 Constitution, Article II, Minutes book page 37.

13 Typewritten history of the Young Woman's Club, n.d.; n.a., History San José.

14 Young Woman's Club annual program, 1903-04.

15 Minutes, 5 October 1916.

16 W. M. Webster, "Floats That Were Covered With Flowers and Blossoms—Exercises At Agricultural Park," *Mercury*, 8 April 1904.

17 "Successful June Festival of Woman's Club," *Mercury*, 25 June 1905.

18 Handwritten notes by Celia (Mrs. Everett) Bailey, 1904.

19 Typewritten history of the Young Woman's Club, n.d.; n.a., History San José.

20 Minutes, 1 May 1913.

21 Ibid., Directors meeting, 14 January 1915.

22 Ibid., 22 and 29 May 1913.

23 Ibid., 1 May 1913.

24 Ibid., Director's meeting, 7 October 1916.

25 Marjorie Pierce, "To Kalon Has Come a Long, Long Way," *Mercury*, n.d. scrapbook, circa 1971.

26 Moore interview.

27 Minutes, 1918.

28 Minutes, 2 May 1918.

29 Typewritten Club Report, dated 22 March 1929.

30 Ibid.

31 Minutes, 23 November 1933.

32 Ibid., 14 December 1933.

33 Beth Lindsay, "Some To Kalon Highlights—From 1903-1953," historical essay prepared for the club, 1978, 8.

34 Minutes, December 1955.

35 Bylaws.

36 Kathryn (Mrs. Allan) Walter, Survey, 2002.

37 *Mercury*, 23 May 1909.

38 Ledger, 1 February 1916.

39 Gere, *Intimate Practices*, 29.

40 Lindsay, 4.

41 Ibid., 1.

42 Minutes, 16 January 1913.

43 Ibid.,1915.

44 Eugene Sawyer, *History of Santa Clara County, California* (Los Angeles: Historic Record Company, 1922), 182.

45 *Mercury*, 12 December 1915, 40.

46 Lindsay, 9.

47 Huette (Mrs. Robert) James, interview with the author, 26 September 2001, Saratoga, California.

48 Marion Langley, interview with the author, 9 February 2001, San José, California.

49 Ibid.

50 Moore interview.

51 Ibid.

52 Betty (Mrs. Richard) Wells, interview with the author, 27 July 2000, San José, California.

53 Rice, *Women, Vol.* 1.

54 Mercury 4 March 1943.

55 Shirley (Mrs. Louis) Oneal, interview with the author, 20 February 2001, San José, California.

56 Elizabeth (Mrs. Arthur) Chinchen , interview with the author, November 2000.

57 Ibid.

58 Ibid.

59 Gerry (Mrs. Robert) Hicks, Survey, 2002.

60 Carol (Mrs. John) Luckhardt. Survey, 2002.

61 Minutes, 1 May 1913.

62 Ibid., 14 December, 1933.

63 Celia (Mrs. Everett) Bailey, Handwritten notes on the club, 4.

64 *Mercury*, 6 November 1910, 26.

65 Minutes, 8 October 1915.

66 Ibid., March 13, 1930.

67 Ibid., 1916.

68 Ibid., 11 February 1915.

69 Marion Langley, "Marion Atkinson Langley Remembers," typewritten essay, 2001.

70 Lindsay, 2.

71 Minutes, October 25, 1934.

72 Scrapbook clipping, 1911, n.p.

73 Ibid., 2.

74 Sue (Mrs. Richard) Casey, Survey, 2002.

75 *Mercury,* 8 August 1897.

76 Scrapbook, 3.

77 Ledger, 1903.

78 *Mercury* 8 February 1906.

79 Jack Douglas, *Historical Footnotes of Santa Clara Valley* (San José: San Jose Historical Museum, 1993), 119.

80 *Mercury,* 4 February 1906

81 Ibid.

82 Mira Abbot Maclay, "Social History Made At Last Night's Brilliant Reception," Ibid., 8 February 1906.

83 Ibid.

84 Celia Bailey, Notes, 5.

85 Ibid., 6.

86 *Mercury*, 11 January 1920, 35/1.

87 Sawyer, *Santa Clara County*, 203.

88 Leonard McKay and Nestor Wahlberg, *A Postcard History of San Jose* (San Jose, CA: Memorabilia, 1992), 94.

89 Patricia Loomis, *Signposts* (San Jose, CA: San Jose Historical Museum, 1982), see photograph, 16.

90 Sawyer, *Santa Clara County*, 224.

91 Elizabeth Evans to Clara (Mrs. Leonard) Edwards, letter, n.d., circa 1960.

92 Celia Bailey, Notes, 6.

93 *Mercury*, 31 May 1908.

94 Clipping scrapbook, May 1918.

95 Marjorie Pierce, clipping, scrapbook, 1971.

96 Nancy Drew to the author, 2001.

97 Mary Bowden Carroll, *Ten Years in Paradise, Leaves From a Society Reporter's Note-book* (San Jose, CA: Popp & Hogan, 1903), 11.

98 Ibid.

99 Loomis, *Signposts*, 91.

100 *Mercury*, 7 April 1930, 6.

101 Joanne Grant, Ibid., 9 August 1992,1B.

102 Ibid., 8.

103 Ibid., 25 February 1917.

104 James interview.

105 Sandy (Mrs. Alex) Stepovich, Survey, 2002.

# Bibliography

## Primary Sources

Bailey, Celia (Mrs. Everett). Handwritten notes 1904-1908.

Evans, Elizabeth to Clara (Mrs. Leonard) Edwards. Letter, n.d., circa 1960.

Langley, Marion. "Marion Atkinson Langley Remembers." Typewritten essay, 2001.

Lindsay, Beth. "Some To Kalon Highlights—From 1903-1953." Historical essay, 1978.

San Jose *Mercury Herald*, *Mercury*, and *Mercury News*, 1900-2002.

To Kalon Club

    Ledgers*

    Minutes*

    Photo Album of current members

    Programs*

    Scrapbook, Volume 2 and 3

    Surveys, 2002

Typewritten Club Report, dated 22 March 1929.

Young Woman's Club

    Ledger*

    Minutes*

    Programs*

    Scrapbook, Volume 1

    Typewritten history of the Young Woman's Club.

## Interviews

    Elizabeth Chinchen

    Nancy Drew

    Huette James

    Marion Langley

    Helen Moore

    Shirley Oneal

    Masel Sheehan

    Betty Wells

## Secondary Sources

Arbuckle, Clyde. *Clyde Arbuckle's History of San Jose*. San Jose: Smith and McKay Printing Company, 1985.

Carroll, Mary Bowden. *Ten Years in Paradise, Leaves From a Society Reporter's Note-book*. San Jose: Popp & Hogan, 1903.

Douglas, Jack. *Historical Footnotes of Santa Clara Valley*. San José: San Jose Historical Museum, 1993.

Gere, Anne Ruggles. *Intimate Practices: Literacy and Cultural Work in U. S. Women's Clubs*. Chicago: University of Illinois Press, 1997.

Loomis, Patricia. *Signposts*. San Jose: San Jose Historical Museum, 1982.

McKay, Leonard and Nestor Wahlberg. *A Postcard History of San Jose*. San Jose: Memorabilia, 1992.

Martin, Theodora Penny. *The Sound of our Own Voices: Women's Study Clubs 1860-1910*. Boston: Beacon Press, 1987.

Rice, Bertha M. *The Women of our Valley, Vol. I*. San Jose: Bertha Rice.

Sawyer, Eugene. *History of Santa Clara County, California*. Los Angeles: Historic Record Company, 1922.

*\* denotes original records stored at History San José*

# Index

*\* Numbers in boldface
type refer to
photographic inserts.*

*Numbers in boldface
type refer to
photographic inserts.*

* Numbers in boldface
   type refer to
   photographic inserts.

*Numbers in boldface type refer to photographic inserts.*

* *Numbers in boldface type refer to photographic inserts.*